PURCHASING STRATEGIES FOR TOTAL QUALITY

A Guide to Achieving Continuous Improvement

THE IRWIN/APICS Series
in Production Management

Supported by the American Production
and Inventory Control Society

OTHER BOOKS PUBLISHED IN THE IRWIN/APICS
SERIES IN PRODUCTION MANAGEMENT

IRWIN/APICS Series in
Production Management

PURCHASING STRATEGIES FOR TOTAL QUALITY
A Guide to Achieving Continuous Improvement

Greg Hutchins
Quality Plus Engineering

IRWIN
Professional Publishing®
Chicago • London • Singapore

Acknowledgments
My sincerest thanks for the
encouragement from Gail
Woodworth, May Stern, and
Jeff Krames.

Greg Hutchins

© RICHARD D. IRWIN, INC. 1992

This publication is designed to provide accurate and authoritative information in
regard to the subject matter covered. It is sold with the understanding that neither
the author nor the publisher is engaged in rendering legal, accounting, or other
professional service. If legal advice or other expert assistance is required, the
services of a competent professional person should be sought.

*From a Declaration of Principles jointly adopted by a Committee of the American Bar
Association and a Committee of Publishers.*

Sponsoring editor:	Jeffrey A. Krames
Project editor:	Gladys True
Production manager:	Carma W. Fazio
Jacket designer:	Michael Finkelman
Compositor:	Carlisle Communications, Ltd.
Typeface:	11/14 Palatino
Printer:	Arcata Graphics/Kingsport

Library of Congress Cataloging-in-Publication Data

Hutchins, Greg.
   Purchasing strategies for total quality : a guide to achieving
continuous improvement / Greg Hutchins.
      p.   cm. — (The Business One Irwin/APICS series in production
management)
   Includes index.
   ISBN 1-55623-380-9
   1. Industrial procurement.   2. Quality of products.   I. Title.
   II. Series.
HD39.5.H88   1991
658.7'2—dc20   90–41990

Printed in the United States of America

2 3 4 5 6 7 8 9 0 AGK 8 7 6

Preface

This book surveys important elements of purchasing quality and competitiveness in the 1990s and beyond. The Cold War is over. International economic competitiveness is assuming more importance. Pundits speculate that competitiveness will be as important in the future as the environmental issue of the 1960s and the energy issue of the 1970s.

Why is this book concerned with competitiveness? This question can be answered through several examples.

In a recent survey conducted by Louis Harris & Associates for *Business Week*, people were asked: "If you had to say, which do you now think is a more serious threat to the future of this country—the military threat from the Soviet Union or the economic threat from Japan?" It is interesting to note that 68 percent perceived the Japanese to be a serious threat compared to 22 percent who were concerned with the Soviet military threat.[1]

In a global economy, quality products sell. Sales produce jobs. Jobs, their creation and maintenance, are the essence of

---

[1] Edited by Mark Vamos, "What Americans Think of Japan Inc," *Business Week*, August 7, 1989, p. 51.

economic development. Economic development is the major public policy issue facing federal, state, county, and municipal governments in the constrained economy of the early 1990s.

The issue of quality is evolving in the purchasing profession and is assuming more importance. Traditionally, industrial and commercial products were purchased based mainly on front-end price, while availability, technology, cost, and service were distant factors in the buy decision. Quality was sometimes not considered. Studies now indicate this has changed. Quality is at the top of most surveys that rank the importance of various factors in the buy decision.

One caveat should be mentioned. I offer examples from Europe and Japan. I do not advocate the wholesale adoption of external management methods, procedures and technologies. If methods are adopted, they must be specifically adapted to the organizational culture, political environment, local tastes, and applicable technology.

The Japanese serve two important purposes. First, they focus public awareness, and create a sense of urgency that I hope will galvanize us to action. Also, the Japanese have established benchmarks against which U.S. firms can measure progress. The goal, however, is not to reach these benchmarks but to surpass them.

A word should be mentioned about the term *customer*. There are three basic types of customers: final, internal, and intermediate. The final customer is the end user of a product or service. The internal customer is the user of a product or service within an organization. In an organization, engineering and purchasing are internal customers of each other. Both share information and resources. In a buyer-seller relationship, the intermediate customer is personified by the purchasing department (the buyer), which distills internal customer's wants, needs, and requirements, and communicates these to the supplier base (the seller). I often refer to the purchasing organization as simply the customer. It should not be confused with the other types of customers, and the term should be understandable in context.

Greg Hutchins
Quality Plus Engineering
Portland, Oregon

Contents

Chapter One
Changing Nature of Purchasing

The global marketplace, technological changes, and other factors are forcing companies to be more competitive. This means satisfying diverse customers with competitively priced, aesthetically pleasing, defect-free products that are delivered in a courteous and timely manner. In essence, companies are trying to satisfy customers with quality products and services.

What does this mean for organizations? Large and small, profit and not-for-profit, manufacturing and service organizations must be customer focused, flexible to adapt to changing market needs, committed to company-wide, continuous improvement, and dedicated to the use of a multidisciplinary approach to provide quality products and services. Product suppliers and service providers to these organizations also should be guided by these principles.

As for employees, they can no longer perform their nominal tasks and expect to homestead jobs until retirement. Each employee, a microcosm of the organization, must be flexible and must continuously upgrade and expand his or her existing skills.

This chapter introduces many of the changes affecting organizations, their suppliers and all employees. The changes listed

TABLE 1–1
Changing Nature of Purchasing Quality

Old Approach	New Approach
Purchasing is tactical issue.	Purchasing is strategic issue.
Price is major factor in buying decision.	Quality is equal to price in buying decision.
Front-end price is important.	Life-cycle costs are critical.
Quality is conformance to specifications.	Quality is broadly defined, mainly in terms of the customer.
Quality is satisfying customer requirements.	Quality is anticipating and exceeding customer expectations.
Purchasing is cost area.	Purchasing is profit/loss area.
Manager supervises function.	Corporate officer leads function.
Products are simple.	Products are complex.
Buyer or agent purchases products.	Team purchases products.
Multiple suppliers provide products.	Preferably single supplier-partner provides products.
Defects are accepted.	Zero defects are expected.
Material quality measured in terms of defect levels.	Material and service quality measured in many ways.
Inspection used to control product quality.	Prevention used to eliminate defects.
Quality is static.	Quality throughout organization and supplier base continuously improves.
Supplier is selected.	Supplier is continuously monitored and evaluated.
Design, manufacturing and purchasing are static.	Design, manufacturing and purchasing are flexible.
Communication is paper based.	Communication is electronically driven.
Product life cycle is long.	Product life cycle is short.
Delivery can be at any time.	Delivery is just-in-time to specific loading dock.

in Table 1–1 are summarized in this chapter and are developed throughout this book.

STRATEGIC AREA

Today's international competitive business environment requires purchasing to focus on world-class manufacturing and sourcing, which are generally acknowledged to be strategic business issues. In many cases, approximately 50 to 80 percent of a firm's manufacturing dollar is spent on supplied material and services. If the percentage is on the lower end of the range, the trend in many companies is to increase the amount of outsourcing. This increase creates a situation where the purchasing manager becomes the de facto manufacturing director, managing the performance of key product suppliers and service providers throughout the development and product life cycles.

QUALITY-MAJOR FACTOR IN DECISION TO BUY

Traditionally, front-end price was the major factor in most commercial and industrial purchase decisions. Often, price consisted of 50 percent or more of the total purchase decision, while product availability, service, and quality were distant factors. Surveys now indicate that measurable elements of quality comprise up to 50 percent or more of the buy decision, while other issues are less important.

LIFE CYCLE COSTS

Many buy decisions are still made on front-end price. Purchasing strategy should focus on the total cost of using, maintaining, and repairing a product through its life, not simply on front-end price. Hidden costs in a defective product, such as the cost of lengthy litigation due to an accident, or the cost of dealing with a dissatisfied customer, can tremendously increase total life cycle costs. This means that the higher front-end priced but more reliable product may represent better overall value.

BROAD QUALITY DEFINITION

At one time, a commonly used definition of quality was conformance to a specification, which was often interpreted as conformance to an engineering print, specification, or standard.If the product conformed to a dimensional tolerance on the print, it was considered acceptable.

In current usage, quality has a much broader definition. Quality is customer and market focused, and integrates many product and service elements, including aesthetics, dimensions, packaging, reliability, durability, features, design, simplicity, delivery, performance, and conformance. In this broader context, the concept of quality affects every organizational area as well as all suppliers. Each area in the customer's and supplier's organization focuses on quality as the means to satisfy the final customer.

From the purchasing perspective, this means that at a minimum, the supplier designs an attractive and safe product; the supplier's manufacturing organization produces a defect-free product; and the supplier's purchasing organization obtains defect-free parts. Furthermore, the supplier has internal management controls and systems to ensure that quality is pursued throughout the organization and with its own suppliers. In essence, the entire supply chain focuses on satisfying and serving the final customer.

ANTICIPATING AND EXCEEDING EXPECTATIONS

For many years, I would have said that serving and satisfying customer wants, needs, and expectations were sufficient to generate profits and maintain customer loyalty. In a recent issue of *The Wall Street Journal*, an advertisement proclaimed that Johnson Control employees wear a special pin as a reminder that their commitment and personal dedication is to *exceed* customer expectations.

Today, I would say that anticipating and exceeding customer wants, needs, and expectations in a cost effective manner is necessary to survive in a global economy.

PROFIT-LOSS AREA

Among the internal elements of an organization, purchasing is a resource and service provider to its own internal clients. To create an internal customer orientation, some organizations are even making purchasing a profit-loss operation. The motive is to create a sense of internal entrepreneurship and a sense of commitment, as well as an impetus for purchasing to serve its internal customers.

CORPORATE LEVEL

As purchasing has become more strategically focused, the principal purchasing position has been raised to corporate officer status. The chief purchasing officer (CPO), often with a vice-presidential title, establishes corporate policies, accountabilities, and objectives for corporate purchasing. At the same time, divisions, independent business units, and plants have the authority and responsibility to purchase the products they use.

In general, the larger the purchasing volume in dollars, amount of material, or technological intensiveness, the higher the purchasing department is in the organization. With an expanded role, purchasing is on the same level as other major functional departments because close coordination is required between purchasing, engineering, manufacturing, and other departments to secure competitively priced, quality products.

COMPLEX PRODUCTS

Products that once were relatively simple are now very complex. Mechanical products have become electronic. Electronic products have become smaller and more complex.

The simple calculator illustrates this trend. Originally, the calculator was a mechanical marvel, bulky and expensive. In its next evolutionary step, the device was big and electronic, and sold for several hundred dollars. The simplest calculator could perform basic arithmetic functions, such as addition, subtraction, multiplication and division.

The simple calculator today has evolved to the point where it is solar-powered, paper-thin, and costs about $20. More expensive models offer a full range of mathematical, statistical, and business functions programmed into their memories. Now, calculators that fit into the palm of a hand have the power of four-year-old desk top personal computers. These units have up to 256,000 bits of memory, enough to perform simple programming, spread sheeting, and word processing.

TEAM APPROACH

Purchasing once had the reputation of serving as an order-taking group. A buyer or agent could be trusted to purchase a product line, a commodity, or a commercial off-the-shelf item. However, as products became more specialized and technical, engineering or some other department would select a product and supplier based upon technical information, and then place an order through purchasing.

Also, engineering would specify products without consulting manufacturing or other internal user groups. This resulted in products that sometimes could not be produced by suppliers or assembled by manufacturing.

During this time, the purchasing person was relegated to drawing up the contract, filling out forms, and passively deferring to technical specialists who had already made the purchasing decision. The purchasing person found himself or herself left out of the communication and negotiation loops.

Many organizations now use a team approach to select and manage suppliers. A team is composed of key individuals from different parts of the organization who are the internal users of the product or service. These people provide the user perspective to the team so that customer requirements are communicated properly to suppliers. Over time, the team integrates key suppliers into the product development team.

SUPPLIER-PARTNER

Quality improvement, Just-In-Time (JIT) delivery, lower cost, technological complexity, and compressed product life cycles have forced greater interdependence between customer and supplier. They have resulted in partnering arrangements with selected single source distributors and suppliers. Partnering is an explicit or implicit arrangement by which selected parties gain more benefits by cooperating in a long-term, win-win relationship than by pursuing a short-term, win-lose arrangement.

Supplier and distributor partnerships are a departure from a relationship that was sometimes adversarial. Adversarial relationships may not have resulted in defective products, but such relationships often resulted in sullen service, posturing, price gouging, or other tactics that inevitably diminished overall quality.

Long-term partnerships with fewer suppliers emphasize mutual trust and communication. Supplier-partners become not only a manufacturing, but also an organizational, extension of the customer. A partner is sometimes expected to have the same type of managerial systems, computer protocols, manufacturing processes, and engineering systems as the customer.

ZERO DEFECTS

Suppliers are expected to produce zero defects or attain parts-per-million (PPM) defect levels. Until recently, it was customary to specify defect levels in terms of parts-per-100 units. This is clearly unacceptable to companies that use supplied parts extensively and want to compete successfully in a global market. Many companies expect suppliers to attain parts-per-million defect levels, and in the near future, parts-per-billion levels.

Regardless of the defect rate, Phil Crosby, an authority on quality and the author of *Quality is Free*, believes that zero defects should be the goal of every manufacturer and supplier. He believes that anything other than this perfect goal communicates a loose standard, which will become the performance benchmark for the supplier.

MEASURING QUALITY AND SERVICE

Several years ago, the main measurement indicators for quality were the number of rejected shipments and the number of defective items in a shipped lot. Service was measured in terms of a subjective appraisal of how well and how quickly the supplier responded to inquiries and provided assistance.

As the quality issue has expanded to involve more organizational areas, supplier quality is now measured in terms of quality costs, delivery, fit, performance, maintainability, and reliability throughout the product life cycle.

PREVENTION ORIENTED

The potential for reducing costs has motivated many companies to become concerned about quality. In the United States, about 15 to 30 percent of each sales dollar goes to ensure that things are done right, and to fix them if they are done wrong. Most of these costs result from warranty claims, field failures, scrap, litigation, and customer dissatisfaction. In contrast, Japan spends only 5 to 10 percent in this area, mainly on preventing defects from occurring.

The only way to improve quality is through prevention, by understanding and controlling the process that produced the product or delivered the service. Thus, the goal of any quality purchaser-supplier partnership is to progress from inspecting product dimensions to ensuring that suppliers start with elementary process controls, and then to evolve into company-wide quality management systems.

Only through statistically based prevention techniques, such as statistical process control (SPC) can parts-per-million quality levels be achieved. For this reason, implementing SPC in key manufacturing areas is the first step in any supplier quality process.

CONTINUOUS IMPROVEMENT

A fundamental element of companywide quality management is a philosophy and commitment to continuous improvement. Every organizational element from accounting to purchasing continuously improves, both to stay competitive and to satisfy the final customer. Since suppliers provide a large proportion of goods and services, suppliers are necessarily a partner in this process.

Continuous supplier improvement starts simply, with a pilot effort in a limited area on a production line, by monitoring a critical or major product quality characteristic. Process variation is monitored, measured, and understood. Key processes are controlled by identifying and eliminating abnormal variation. In time, statistical process control (SPC) and other prevention technologies are expanded to more production areas, and statistical analysis is moved upstream into technical, professional, and administrative areas.

CONTINUOUS EVALUATION AND MONITORING

At one time, if a supplier produced a reasonably good product, the supplier could expect to retain a manufacturer's business for many years. Perhaps each year, the supplier's sales representative and a buyer would go through a negotiation ritual where each would try to secure the most favorable terms on price or delivery. At the end of the dance, a deal would be struck and both parties would retire to a favorite watering hole to celebrate the deal. This ritual was repeated yearly.

Today, negotiations emphasize continuous improvement, integration of capabilities, open communication, and mutual trust. Suppliers are extensively and intensively evaluated and monitored before they are chosen as partners. And, if problems arise, corrective action is immediately initiated to remove the symptom and eliminate the root cause.

FLEXIBLE DESIGN, MANUFACTURING, AND PURCHASING

Design, manufacturing, and supplier flexibility is necessary to accommodate and satisfy special or specific customer requirements quickly. This means that a small number of products, or even one product with specific quality attributes, can be produced quickly to satisfy a special customer order. Supplier-partners, as an extension of the customer's manufacturing facility, are expected to participate in responding to these special needs.

The ability to target, satisfy, and quickly respond to specific customers can only be accomplished through integrated and controlled processes. For example, machines can be quickly set up for different size production runs. A machine can be programmed to produce one product with specific quality characteristics, and then quickly adjusted to produce a product for another customer with different requirements.

ELECTRONIC COMMUNICATION

Paperwork, labor-intensive routine transactions, clerical time, data entry, and mailing costs are overwhelming organizations. And every time information is manually duplicated, the chance of human error increases.

To gain a market advantage, many firms are using electronic data interchange (EDI) to share information about demand patterns, inventory levels, production plans, and quality information. EDI is the intercompany and intracompany transmission of business documents in a standard format. Quotes, quality information, purchase orders, production schedules, billing, and invoice statements can be communicated in this fashion. EDI is particularly being used by companies having a large volume of recurring business transactions that require timely and accurate data tracking, processing, and reporting. EDI thus eliminates duplication, lost information, and mistaken orders. EDI is really the first step in the evolution to seamless intercompany and intracompany communications network.

SHORT PRODUCT LIFE CYCLE

The product life cycle (PLC) is composed of four parts: introduction, growth, maturity, and decline. For many products, the PLC was once five years or more. Now, with technological changes and fickle consumer tastes, the PLC for these same products is two years or less. Thus, organizations and their suppliers must anticipate market trends and satisfy customers quickly.

Supplier-partners are selected carefully and integrated into the customer's product development team. Otherwise, problems may occur. The old school business practice was that suppliers were selected when production was about to begin. Drawings were sent to the hastily chosen supplier, who was expected to produce quality products consistently and to deliver them just in time to be used by the customer. The supplier had little time to prepare and to fully understand customer requirements. This process was sometimes disastrous.

When a PLC is short, a manufacturer does not have the time to design a product and then find world-class suppliers to produce key components or assemblies. A supplier may not have sufficient time, engineering expertise, or production capabilities to make the new product. Also, a world-class supplier already may have promised production to other customers and may have no room for expansion. The solution is to integrate key suppliers into product development.

JIT DELIVERY

In the narrow sense, Just-In-Time (JIT) purchasing calls for the reduction of inventory by having required materials available at each point in the manufacturing process, just-in-time to be used. In a broader sense, JIT is a philosophy of management excellence that seeks to eliminate all types of waste and facilitate material movement.

Customer-supplier JIT interaction is most intense at the operations or plant level. At the plant level, key suppliers are sometimes called daily about quality levels, delivery targets, packaging, shipping, and special requests. In some automotive JIT plants, suppliers drop ship key parts to different plant locations two or more times a day. Early shipments mean that trucks may wait idling, and late shipments may stall an assembly operation.

Many companies adopt JIT manufacturing principles without fully understanding their implications. For example, JIT requires defect-free material from suppliers. In the worst case, a shipment of defective parts can shut down a production line unless there is sufficient buffer inventory. But one of the guiding principles behind JIT is that all inventories are drastically reduced and preferably eliminated.

The next chapter discusses how changes in the global economy are giving rise to the issues discussed in this chapter.

Chapter Two
Global Competitiveness

The changes discussed in the last chapter are occurring because of the accelerating integration of the world's economic activities. The global marketplace has become almost a cliché. Markets, heretofore closed, are opening. The Soviet Union and the nations of Eastern Europe are widening their business contacts with the West and seeking favorable trading status. An integrated Europe is lowering tariffs and trade barriers. Pacific Rim countries are leveling their playing fields and encouraging the entry of foreign made goods.

A unified Europe may well become the most potent economic entity in the 1990s. The European Community (E.C.) is working to eliminate nontariff trade barriers among the 12 member countries by December 1992. E.C. members already have agreed to a system of mutual recognition that will allow a product tested and certified in one country to be admitted to other E.C. markets, assuming the product meets basic health, safety, and quality standards.

In anticipation of a much more competitive European market, many non-European firms are already establishing European operations to manufacture, design, source, and conduct research and development (R&D) within the E.C. U.S. companies are positioning themselves by compiling current information about the E.C. market's progress, auditing European operations, and marketing and fine-tuning each operation to satisfy different European customer requirements.[1] Companies that cannot or do not follow these options are teaming up with European partners.

U.S. AUTO INDUSTRY

Not too many years ago, U.S. companies dominated world markets in most goods and services. But increasing global competition has dramatically changed most domestic markets. Now, Pacific Rim and European companies dominate the consumer electronics, steel, auto, computer, and other markets. In addition, foreign competitors have penetrated service markets such as banking, movies, retailing, and transportation. These pressures are or will soon become part of every organization's business landscape, whether these businesses are service or manufacturing, or large or small organizations.

The U.S. auto industry felt the impact of the emerging global economy and its competitive pressures in the early 1980s. The Big Three automakers owned the domestic auto market and were largely complacent until they started losing a significant share of this market. The challenges faced by America's Big Three automakers (G.M., Ford, and Chrysler) and their responses illustrate the risks that most firms will face in the 1990s.

The U.S. automobile market has become even more competitive in the last few years with the domestic manufacturing of Japanese autos. Nissan, Honda, Mazda, Toyota, and Mitsubishi have transplanted entire fabrication, assembly, and supplier networks to the United States. These networks are tightly integrated and produce cars of superior quality, reliability, performance, and style. Detroit is now scared and is beginning to emulate the designing, manufacturing, and sourcing methods of these upstart competitors.

VERTICAL INTEGRATION

For many years, auto makers followed a strategy of vertical integration, thereby controlling the entire design, production, and distribution process. Little was purchased, and everything related to building cars was done in-house. Conventional wisdom said that if a company owned the sources of raw material, processed the raw material, designed the products, machined, fabricated, marketed, and finally distributed the product, profits and market-share would be assured. Vertical integration offered the advantages of standardization of products; control of operating, marketing, and distribution channels; and size, and cost efficiencies.

This philosophy however, may not work as well in a global, disaggregated economy. In such a market, no company, not even a multinational conglomerate, has the resources to be the best in each element of the business, and to be all things to all people. This is especially true in an economy characterized by small, discrete markets.

Markets are becoming more segmented, so that at some point, the eventual market may conceivably be the individual. In other words, an individual will have his or her needs, wants, and expectations satisfied by a tailored product or service. The individual consumer may be able to specify preferences through an interactive television connected directly to the product manufacturer. The manufacturer will then communicate customer requirements directly to a cell of production machines, which will produce a product with the quality characteristics required by the customer. In this way, entire marketing and distribution chains will be bypassed.

MOVING AWAY FROM VERTICAL INTEGRATION

Vertical integration is losing its appeal in favor of such arrangements as strategic alliances, joint ventures, or partnerships. Global competition, high product development costs, high product and service quality expectations, shortened product life cycles, and rapidly changing market requirements encourage companies to form alliances and partnerships. Simply stated, partnering is a process in which two or more companies cooperate to a high degree to achieve separate but complementary objectives.

Partnering offers many of the advantages of vertical integration without the concomitant risks. One major advantage of partnering has been to make companies more flexible by allowing them to satisfy different customers with economical, quality products and services. Other partnering advantages include risk sharing; manufacturing and design flexibility; and access to markets, information, capital, and other resources. Simply put, companies focus on factors in which they have an edge and seek partners that offer expertise, knowledge, or resources in areas where they aren't as strong.[2]

Why doesn't one company simply buy a controlling stake in the prospective partner and learn its methods? Buying a company and thereby obtaining its proprietary knowledge does not buy the entrepreneur's loyalty, drive, and future ideas. On the other hand, a partnership accesses the other party's distinct advantages without jeopardizing the vital energy and entrepreneurial dream that produced the breakthrough in the first place.

Partnerships are also synergistic. The results of the partnership offer each party more than they would have gained individually. In addition, technology and the character of markets are changing so rapidly that companies must be driven, hungry, and adaptable to change. Equity ownership encourages people with vision to assume risks as they seek to improve their economic status.

Partnering takes several forms:

- Technology sharing.
- Marketing and production alliances.
- Product and service alliances.
- Supplier partnering.

Technology Sharing
In this type of collaboration, the goal is to offer a unique capability in exchange for acquisition of the rights to joint research.

The unique capability may be research or development expertise, a proprietary product, distinct engineering capabilities, or specialized manufacturing expertise. In a recent public-private collaboration, Du Pont, Hewlett-Packard, and Los Alamos National Laboratory collaborated on a three-year, $11 million superconductor research project. The materials discovered in this research conduct electricity with low resistance, which should allow for smaller, faster computers.[3]

Marketing and Production Alliances

As shown in Table 2–1, marketing and production alliances are reshaping the global automotive industry. U.S. automakers now buy vehicles from non-U.S. manufacturers to satisfy certain domestic market niches with captive imports. The automakers expect to cut costs by buying and reselling compact and subcompact models, instead of manufacturing them, because small models don't have the profit margins of larger autos. The automaker and customer both benefit. The automaker boosts profits while the customer has more automotive choices.[4]

Product and Service Alliances

Even giants such as IBM are partnering to provide customized systems solutions that involve joint products and services. IBM, serving as a broker, identifies a customer problem and proposes a solution involving itself and a service provider that has in-depth industry or application knowledge.

Historically, IBM provided all the solutions, but now the company realizes that even its prodigious size and available expertise cannot provide all customers with solutions to all problems. What's the win for IBM? IBM provides the hardware and may provide the software, while the partner fits the hardware and customizes the software for a particular application.[5]

Supplier Partnering

Supplier partnering is another form of the global trend toward strategic alliances that mutually favor the buyer and a key

TABLE 2–1
Global Partnering among the Big Three

General Motors	Ford Motor Co.	Chrysler Corp.
Cadillac	Ford	Dodge
Chevrolet	Mercury	Plymouth
(Geo and Lumina)	Lincoln	Chrysler
Buick	*United Kingdom*	*United States*
Oldsmobile	Aston Martin	Owns 50% of
Pontiac	Owns 77% of Jaguar	Diamond Star
United States	*Europe*	Motors with
Owns 50% of NUMMI	Ford of Europe	Mitsubishi
with Toyota (Geo	*Japan*	*Italy*
Prism)	Owns 25% of Mazda	Lamborghini
Owns 24% of a	*South Korea*	Owns 16% of Maserati
joint venture with	Owns 11% of Kia	Owns 50% with Fiat of
Volvo	*Brazil*	distribution rights to
United Kingdom	Owns 49% of joint	Alpha Romeo in
Lotus	venture with	U.S.
Vauxhall	Volkswagen	*Japan*
Owns 60% of a joint	*Australia*	Owns 12% of
venture w/Isuzu	Ford of Australia	Mitsubishi
Europe		*France*
Opel		Owns 50% of ARAC
Owns 50% of Saab		with Renault
(auto division)		*Egypt*
Owns 50% of joint		Own 49% of Arab GM
venture with Raba		American vehicles
South America		*China*
GM do Brasil		Owns 31% of Beijing
Australia		Automotive Works
Owns 50% of joint		*Canada*
venture with Toyota		Is pursuing joint
Japan		venture with
Owns 40% of Isuzu		Hyundai to produce
Owns 5% of Suzuki		4-door Eagles in
Korea		1991
Owns 50% of Daewoo		
Motor Co.		

Reprinted with permission from the Auto Show Supplement, "Brothers Under the Hood," *Willamette Week.* January 25–31, 1990, p. 180.

supplier. Most joint-supplier agreements focus on one specialty product or a high volume line. This subject will be developed throughout this book.

PRODUCT DEVELOPMENT PARTNERSHIPS

As products become more technical and individually customized, the future global business entity may well be small, interlocking entrepreneurial companies that jointly develop a product. These may well be the prototypical, world-class suppliers that everyone will want. One company may have engineering skills. Others may have marketing, financial, and other essential skills. The entrepreneurial businesses will be run by people of vision and intelligent risk taking.

These small, entrepreneurial companies will be able to produce and deliver world-class products and services in narrowly defined markets. They will be nimble, able to respond quickly to market conditions. They will have instant access to information, be able to recognize market niche advantages, and have the ability to adapt and accommodate quickly by delivering customized products. The trick will be to unify these disparate and unique organizations.

Product-development partnerships will not have to last forever or be exclusive. They may be customized to accommodate the needs and abilities of each party, thus allowing each partner to pursue objectives with other firms.

RESPONSES

Today, global changes are forcing every organization, supplier, and employee to do things differently and to improve continuously in order to satisfy the final customer. In general, there is a worldwide production over capacity for most products. The world is becoming a buyer's market for every industrial, commercial, and consumer product.

An increasingly rare occurrence is that a special application, or proprietary product, may still own an exclusive marketplace niche. And if the product is not updated periodically, another technology or emulator will try to capture the exclusive market. In the quest for efficiency and competitiveness, companies worldwide are changing the ways in which products are manufactured and materials are purchased.

SERVE THE CUSTOMER

Serving the customer is universally acknowledged as a basic principle of excellent management. Serving the customer means not only satisfying present wants and needs, but also anticipating and satisfying expectations. Satisfying expectations requires a certain amount of crystal ball gazing. In many industries, especially in those related to consumer products and fashions, the mood of the customer must be anticipated one to two years in advance.

In this marketplace, innovative, attractive, competitively priced world-class products and services sell. Products are made to satisfy specific national, ethnic, or geographic tastes. Products are continuously updated. Supplier base is dramatically reduced. The importance of price declines in favor of quality. Production runs must necessarily be short.

DO WHAT YOU DO BEST

Originally, a factory produced one product that satisfied a set of customers. As customer needs changed, the plant incorporated new machinery, organized into new processes, to produce new products. Over time, existing products were updated and new products were developed.

Multiproduct plants became a jigsaw puzzle of unrelated processes and machinery. Each new product line added new machinery, new inventory, and parallel cost systems. The plants became complex and inflexible. These multiproduct plants created additional sources of variation, which as you will discover in the next chapter, is a prescription for increased defects and inevitably, lower customer satisfaction.

Organizations discovered that it was impossible to be the best in everything or to be all things to all people. Recently, the trend towards excellence is pushing companies to emphasize what they do well, which means focusing on one product or on a narrow product line. Parallel and complex systems are eliminated. All work the company is not excellent at is contracted to single-source, world-class suppliers. These narrowly focused suppliers have dedicated equipment, machinery, systems, and people to concentrate on satisfying the demands of one set of customers.

This philosophy means doing all high-quality, low-cost work in-house, and outsourcing all other work. This make or buy decision generally leads to a large percentage, up to 80 percent, of the manufacturing dollar being outsourced.

The philosophy of doing what one does best also means that key suppliers are encouraged and induced to integrate manufacturing and engineering systems with those of the customer. Doing a customer's high value-added work requires that suppliers become very knowledgeable of the customer's systems, processes, and products. For example, if a supplier designs a critical subassembly, it must know how each subassembly functions with lower order components as well as with higher order assemblies.

SUPPLIER PARTNERING

HP buys aluminum stock from three suppliers compared to 22 five years ago.[6]

GM evaluated 400 suppliers before paring the list to 69 primary suppliers for its new quad 4 engine program.[7]

Tenant has the goal of reducing the supplier base by 10 percent per year.[8]

As the above news items illustrate, the 1990s will see growing competition among suppliers to retain the business of large corporations. The global market is already saturated with production capacity and as developing countries build additional capacity, the marketplace will become even more customer driven. Industrial buyers will be able to pick and choose those supplier-partners they want to work with based on quality, cost, technology, and service criteria.[9]

SUPPLIER QUALITY PARTNERING

Again, the first indications of the need for better quality were seen in the auto industry. Knowing that 60 to 75 percent of a customer's satisfaction with a vehicle depends on its quality, the Big Three became quality driven. The Big Three automakers also knew that a large percent of their manufacturing dollar was being outsourced. So if they wanted to control, assure, and manage the quality of their final products, they had to encourage their suppliers and their suppliers' suppliers to adopt the same type of quality systems.

In the brutally competitive domestic auto market of the second half of the 1980s, the Big Three automakers and their suppliers felt growing pressure of the Japanese transplants. The pressure will continue throughout the 1990s as these transplants assert quality internally and with all suppliers. They are aiming to see that most parts and commodities are eventually single sourced.

Ford Motor Co.'s supplier-quality standard, Q-101, (discussed in Chapter 4) became a template for many early supplier-quality efforts. Before awarding a supplier its Q1 certification, the supplier's management, manufacturing capability, engineering capability, gauging, quality, technical capability, delivery, and worldwide cost competitiveness are evaluated. Chrysler Corp. and General Motors also have developed similar quality standards.

These quality standards have similar goals: to improve product and service quality; lower overall costs; improve product delivery; and increase customer satisfaction. Suppliers are intensively and extensively evaluated until only the best suppliers become preferred "ship to assembly" supplier-partners. Obviously, the supplier base is drastically cut. For example, GM's stated goal is to reduce 40 percent of its existing supplier base and to favor supplier-partners.

Supplier continuous improvement efforts have resulted in more parts conforming to specifications, reduced vehicle manufacturing costs, lowered engineering costs, and reduced supplier base. These critical improvements translated into important measures of customer loyalty and market share. From 1980 to 1988, Ford Motor Company increased customer loyalty from 35 percent to 47 percent, which was the largest increase among domestic auto manufacturers. This was also reflected in market share increases for Ford from 16.9 percent in 1982 to 21.3 percent at the end of the 1988 model year.[10]

Supplier partnering is a natural outgrowth of the collaborating and joint venturing that occurs in the global economy. For many products, companies will form and develop mutually beneficial, long-term strategic partnerships with one key supplier, or a key supplier and an acceptable alternate. Recently, General Motors (GM) and Ford Motor Company executives reported that 98 percent of their automotive parts made by outside suppliers were single sourced.[11]

PARTNERS AS STAKEHOLDERS

One of the earliest references to partnering and creating value was a piece in NCR Corporation's mission statement. NCR calls its partners *stakeholders*. The first page of NCR's 1986 annual report states: "We think of our suppliers as partners who share our goal of achieving the highest quality standards and the most consistent level of service."

NCR puts suppliers on the same level as other stakeholders, including employees, management, stockholders, and customers. These people have a vested interest in the ability of NCR to create value. NCR believes the ability to create value for each stakeholder group has helped NCR be successful in the marketplace. In the near future, most companies will perceive their key suppliers in the same manner.

CONTINUOUS IMPROVEMENT

Companywide continuous improvement is a hallmark of every customer-supplier partnership. Continuous improvement is a proactive approach to prevent problems from occurring rather than detecting and then correcting them after they occur. Companywide continuous improvement is essential to achieving many business goals, whether they involve quality, delivery, service, cost, or technology competitiveness. Continuous improvement affects every organizational element, including management, employees, distributors, and suppliers that are involved in creating value by designing, producing, or delivering a product or service to the final customer.

Continuous improvement requires a change in mind set. Traditionally, most U.S. organizations focused on product innovation to remain competitive. While innovation is still important, the emphasis is shifting to the processes that develop a product, from designing it, producing it, and supplying components, to delivering service.

Continuous improvement is evolving into an ethic or culture in many organizations. Continuous improvement is an organizational mindset whereby small, incremental, day-to-day operational changes are often the result of individual and group initiatives. On the other hand, innovation is the result of a major change. Innovation may be the invention of a new product, discovery of a scientific truth, or a significant investment in new technology.

The differences between innovation and continuous improvement have been compared to hitting an infrequent home run and hitting consistent singles. It is becoming accepted that to win the competitiveness game, a series of consistent single improvements will win over the inconsistent home run. Similarly, pundits speculate the reason why Japanese firms are more competitive than similar U.S. firms is because of our penchant for the short-term home run instead of the long-term series of singles.[12]

There are other implications, as shown in Table 2–2. Innovation represents a quantum leap in knowledge. The person responsible for innovation achieves recognition and honors. Also, innovation is risky, requiring development time, specialized knowledge and contributions of many experts, and often research and development facilities.

Continuous improvement is not a technical issue so much as an organizational and management issue. Continuous improvement is a group activity that focuses, integrates, and implements the knowledge and expertise of individuals in the group. It does not require much money. It can be done by

TABLE 2–2
Continuous Improvement versus Innovation

Feature	Continuous Improvement	Innovation
Focus	Problems are opportunities for improvement.	Problems reflect management abilities.
Management	Functions to support and stimulate improvement by removing organizational roadblocks.	Directive and judgmental.
Involvement	All personnel functioning as teams and as individuals.	Top management and experts.
Practical requirements	Requires little investment but great effort to maintain.	Requires large investment but little effort to maintain.

Targets for Excellence, Detroit: General Motors Corp., 1987, pp. 1–6.

anyone or by any team committed to eliminating waste and excessive variation.

LONG-TERM PERSPECTIVE

Continuous improvement requires a long-term perspective. A supplier should not implement quality techniques on impulse or in the hope of retaining business.

At GM, continuous improvement is an organizational philosophy based on how the company wants to conduct business. GM. tells its internal and external suppliers that they are expected to adopt a similar incremental improvement philosophy if they want to retain GM's long term business.

In its continuous improvement drive, GM management has three major functions. First, management develops goals and strategies to assure continuous improvement by involving all elements and all organizational levels. These goals result in process standards. Second, management assures that process standards are current, achievable, and measurable. Third, management develops a system to evaluate and improve these standards periodically.

WORLD CLASS SUPPLIERS

The immediate objective of continuous improvement is a satisfied customer. The longer term goal is to achieve increased competitiveness in the global marketplace.

What does this mean specifically? To Motorola, a 1988 Malcolm Baldrige National Quality Award winner, total customer satisfaction is the organization's fundamental objective. Motorola attributes its competitive success to helping its management, employees, and suppliers clearly understand that if total customer satisfaction is pursued and achieved through continuous improvement, everything else will necessarily follow. Important daily operational crises and roadblocks are always solvable if it is universally understood that they result from a failure to totally satisfy the internal or external customer.[13]

Because of overuse, the words *competitiveness* and *world-class* also have become clichés. Not so, however, to organizations that must compete against Pacific Rim and European goliaths. Competitiveness is a visceral survival issue. Again, at Motorola competitiveness means:

1. Increased global market share.
2. Best in a class in terms of people, technology, marketing product, manufacturing, and service.
3. Superior financial results.[14]

Motorola communicates this message to its suppliers. It requires its suppliers to apply for the National Quality Award or be dropped from the company's approved suppliers' list. This is a tough message for tough times.

CONTINUOUS SUPPLIER IMPROVEMENT

To prosper in the competitive 1990s, continuous supplier improvement will evolve into conventional management wisdom.

To the Ford Motor Company, continuous supplier improvement means that internal and external suppliers strive to achieve the following goals:

- Understand and improve organizational systems and processes.
- Use statistical process control in measuring performance of quality criteria.
- Establish targets for significant process and product characteristics and reduce variation around these targets.
- Obtain timely internal and external customer feedback data.
- Establish a rating system and measure customer perceptions of products and services.
- Identify principal and best-in-class competition to assess the quality of processes, products, and services.
- Develop a cost of quality system.
- Educate employees in quality.
- Assist customers and suppliers, as partners, to improve the quality of their products and services.[15]

The following chapters will discuss and detail how suppliers are adopting the above precepts of excellence.

NOTES

[1]Kate Bertrand, "Scrambling for 1992," *Business Marketing*, February 1989, pp. 48–59.

[2]John Thackray, "America's Vertical Cutback," *Management Today*, June 1986, pp. 74–76.

[3]"Du Pont, Hewlett-Packard Set Superconductor Effort," *Wall Street Journal*, November 7, 1989, p. B4.

[4]William Hampton, "Downsizing Detroit: The Big Three's Strategy for Survival," *Business Week*, April 14, 1986, pp. 86–88.

[5]"The Problem: The Solution," ad in the *Wall Street Journal*, December 13, 1989, p. B4.

[6]Purchasing, September 24, 1987, p. 51.

[7]Purchasing, September 24, 1987, p. 51.

[8]Purchasing, September 24, 1987, p. 51.

[9]Early research, work, and writing on supplier partnering was done by David Burt.

[10]Todd Englander, "Ford: Quality Driven," *Incentive*, Jan. 1989, pp. 23–24.

[11]John Sheridan, "Betting On a Single Source," *Industry Week*, February 1, 1988, pp. 31–36.

[12]The analogy of continuous improvement being a series of singles is not mine. I've forgotten the original source.

[13]This was derived from a casestudy, "The Motorola Story," submitted by Motorola to National Institute for Standards and Technology on its successful effort to win the Malcolm Baldrige Quality Award.

[14]This was derived from a casestudy, "The Motorola Story," submitted by Motorola to National Institute for Standards and Technology on its successful effort to win the Malcolm Baldrige Quality Award.

[15]"Total Quality Excellence Award Program," Ford Motor Company, p. 3.

Chapter Three
Controlling and Improving Quality

T he purpose of this chapter is to define various elements and perspectives of quality, and then discuss how continuous improvement is achieved through controlling variation and preventing defects from occurring through statistical process control (SPC).

Quality is a multidimensional word. The definition of quality has expanded as the function has evolved from inspection to quality control, quality assurance, and companywide quality management.

Its usage now encompasses elements that were never before associated with the word. At first, quality was defined as conformance to specifications. The definition then expanded to incorporate the concepts of customer satisfaction, service quality, and companywide and supplierwide continuous improvement. In a global context, quality is now defined as doing what needs to be done to maintain and improve competitiveness.

Three basic perspectives of quality are commonly encountered:

- Marketing.
- Value.
- Engineering and manufacturing.[1]

MARKETING

The marketing perspective of quality is user or customer based. Quality is defined as the ability to satisfy a customer's wants, needs, and expectations. The customer can be internal or external to the organization.

At one time, a firm could profit by satisfying some combination of wants and needs. This situation has changed. With the fast pace of technological change, brief product life cycles and fickle tastes, companies must anticipate and satisfy customer expectations. Satisfying expectations requires a certain amount of crystal ball gazing.

Also, if the highest product quality is not delivered in a courteous manner, the customer's perception of the product will probably be marred and remain that way. Attributes related to quality, around which service standards have been designed, incorporate such elements as courtesy, security, consistency, attitude, delivery, availability, completeness, and timing.[2]

VALUE

These days, more products are quality made and quality serviced. Products made in newly developing countries that have relatively low labor and raw material costs are of increasingly high quality. In the future, customers will no longer be simply satisfied with quality products and services. Because once satisfied, customer expectations tend to rise to incorporate more quality related elements.

So what will satisfy customers in the future? The answer will involve the customer's entire experience with the product, including: an aesthetically pleasing package; a competitively priced, reliable and maintainable product; and a prompt and courteous system of delivery and service. Products will necessarily be designed and customized to an individual's requirements. They will be introduced in the marketplace quickly. They will be continuously updated throughout their short product life cycles.

This value perspective of quality is becoming more prevalent. Succinctly, value is the optimum blend of quality, service, and price, so that the customer, producer, and supplier are all satisfied. Implicit in this broadened definition is the idea that while the customer is happy, the product manufacturer, service provider, and product supplier are also satisfied because they have sufficient profit motive to want to continue to satisfy the final customer.

Value creation may be illustrated by the evolution of the 5¼ inch computer floppy disk. When personal computers were an early novelty, floppy disks were high priced. A computer disk simply stores information in magnetized particles spread over a piece of plastic. A disk is now so prevalent and standardized that it has become a commodity. It is amazingly cheap and durable. The general quality of any floppy disk is high in terms of meeting specifications and satisfying the customer.

Several years ago, disk manufacturers wanted to differentiate their products from others. So, they added value by providing additional customer support and attractive packaging. One manufacturer promised service anywhere in the world within 24 hours. Another sold products in fancy colored packages. Floppy disks that once were IBM grey or Apple beige were enclosed in colored packages. Why color? Colored disks helped customers to organize information better than beige color packages.[3]

Over the long haul, how is value created and sustained? A major way is through internal partnering, such as employee involvement, and through similar programs as external partnering. This is exemplified by NCR Corporation's six mission statements, which emphasize value creation by its major stakeholders:

- Business activity is conducted with integrity and respect by building mutually beneficial and enduring relationships with all stakeholders.
- Customer satisfaction is taken personally.
- The individuality of each employee is respected and employee creativity and productivity are encouraged and rewarded.
- Suppliers are thought of as partners.

- There is a commitment to being caring and supportive corporate citizens in communities in which NCR operates.
- The firm is dedicated to creating value for shareholder and financial communities.[4]

ENGINEERING AND MANUFACTURING

Once customer wants, needs, and expectations are understood, an engineering team develops understandable, realistic, complete, usable, and measurable specifications. It is generally thought that engineering drawings and other documents specify a product's physical dimensions. These documents can also spell out other quality related factors, such as: performance, critical quality characteristics, reliability, dimensional stability, quality levels, features, maintainability, packaging, durability, fit, and finish.[5] For special products or for service, other quality attributes or factors may be specified. For example, software quality criteria may include correctness, efficiency, reliability, flexibility, completeness, traceability, system complexity, and maintenance.[6]

Even the most mundane and seemingly simple specifications can be complicated. For example, the computer paper used in a laser printer can affect final product quality and inevitably, customer satisfaction. Some specifications and terms used to specify paper include: opacity, finish, chemistry, substance weight, and cotton content.

Once, critical quality characteristics have been defined, then they have to be controlled. This raises the issue of variation, which is dealt with in the next section. The management of quality is sometimes called the study of variation because excessive variation in any process, whether administrative, service, or manufacturing, can cause quality to deteriorate. For example, too much variation in the above paper properties can cause printers to malfunction. In essence, quality control is the ability to consistently meet a specification target and then to improve continuously by minimizing variation about the specification target.

STATISTICAL PROCESS CONTROL

Five years ago, incoming material shipments consisting of 95 percent conforming products were considered acceptable. Today, many suppliers must provide products that are 99.9 percent conforming, which is still 1,000 parts per million (PPM) nonconforming. This is clearly unacceptable in many industries that require suppliers to achieve 3 or 4 PPM defect levels.

PPM defect or zero defect levels cannot be inspected into a product. Defects and flaws must be prevented from occurring by moving responsibility for quality upstream into the supplier's engineering and manufacturing departments.

Basically, SPC is a technique to prevent defects from occurring while a product is being produced. Instead of inspecting product dimensions at the customer's receiving dock, responsibility for quality is moving to the supplier's manufacturing process. The assumption is that if the supplier's process is running satisfactorily and is capable of meeting specifications, the products coming out of the process conform to specifications. In general, SPC informs the customer that the supplier is monitoring and controlling key manufacturing processes. However, SPC should not be seen as an end in itself, but only as a first step in a long-term process of continuous improvement.

PROCESS CONCEPT

Service or product quality can be consistently delivered only if it is defined, checked, and controlled along each step of the process. This means all the way from marketing to determine customer requirements; to engineering and designing an aesthetic, reliable product; to purchasing and obtaining defect-free parts; to manufacturing and assembling these parts correctly; and to sales personnel being courteous and responsive to customer concerns.

This value creation chain consists of a series of integrated process steps in which each step adds or detracts product value. Basically, a process is a particular method of performing an operation and consists of a series of sequential steps. Each

FIGURE 3–1
Inspection versus Process Control

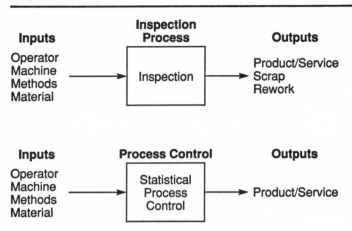

step adds value to the product or service. For example, if a production process step shows excessive variation because the raw material is inconsistent, the method of machining is not specified, the operator is sloppy, or the machine cannot meet specifications, then final product quality will subsequently vary and value is detracted. If the output of each process step is inspected, then the outputs can be acceptable products, scrap, or rework. If variation in each process step is monitored and controlled, then the output is an acceptable product or service as shown in Figure 3–1.

SPC can also be used to understand and reduce variation in an administrative area. An administrative process consists of procedures, policies, supervision, people, equipment, and supplies. When one or more of these factors is inconsistent or shows wide variation, service quality also deteriorates.

MANAGEMENT BY EXCEPTION

SPC in some ways is analogous to management by exception. An administrative or manufacturing process runs naturally until an abnormal event occurs. At this point, the operator evaluates the event and if the operator concludes the event is random and a normal part of the process, then nothing is done. If the event has an identifiable cause, the event is considered abnormal, and the operator tries to understand the nature of the cause in order to eliminate it.

Once abnormal causes have been eliminated, a system is considered stable and under control. An administrative example may clarify this. An administrative assistant handles routine, administrative purchasing issues until there is an abnormal condition, an exception to the regular work flow. First, the administrative assistant tries to fix the problem, which may mean reconciling numbers on a ledger. If this settles the matter, it goes no further. If the problem recurs and the administrative assistant cannot change the fundamental process that causes the errors, then a supervisor may have to authorize additional training, eliminate an upstream cause, or develop new internal procedures. The process is similar in manufacturing.

FUNDAMENTALS OF STATISTICAL PROCESS CONTROL

Essentially, SPC provides evidence that a shipment of incoming products conforms to specifications and the process producing the products is running naturally. SPC is based on the following basic ideas:

- Quality is conformance to specifications.
- Processes and products vary.
- Variation in processes and products can be measured.
- Normal variation follows a bell shaped curve.
- Abnormal variation distorts the bell shape.
- Causes of variation can be isolated and identified.[7]

QUALITY IS CONFORMANCE TO SPECIFICATIONS

An organization first determines the requirements and expectations of the final customer. Several methods commonly used are:

- Customer interviews.
- Customer surveys.

- Field service reports.
- Quality studies.
- Warranty reports.
- Field return reports.
- Nonconforming material reports.
- Product audits.
- Quality function deployment.

Based on the results of the survey, engineering then develops a set of specifications for the entire product, and then for its assemblies, subassemblies, systems, subsystems, and components. Engineering may also specify how each of these systems will be made. Specifications at the product level can detail acceptable levels of performance, reliability, maintainability, serviceability, appearance, ease of use, or safety. At the component level, specifications can detail acceptable dimensions, fit, and interaction of components. Specifications for a complex product may consist of thousands of pages.

PRODUCTS AND PROCESSES VARY

In manufacturing, no two machines are the same. Even two parts made from the same machine are not identical. There is always some variation, which may only be detected at the microscopic level.

As was mentioned, the control and assurance of quality is the study of variation. In a production process, it is the study of the dispersion of measurements in a product quality characteristic. Many statistical studies in manufacturing and business have shown that measured data have a tendency to cluster around a measurement point and be dispersed around this point, as shown in Figure 3–2.

VARIATION CAN BE MEASURED

Variation can be detected and measured by critical measuring instruments, some of which can measure a dimension to a millionth of an inch until variation is detected. To ensure that external factors don't influence the measurement, critical mea-

FIGURE 3–2
Measured Values Cluster Around 0.500 Inches

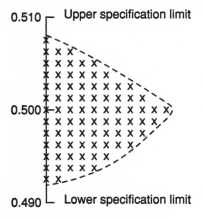

x = Measured value
0.500" ± 0.010" = Specification spread

surements may be performed in special rooms where humidity, particulates, and temperature are carefully controlled.

NORMAL VARIATION IN MEASUREMENTS FOLLOWS A BELL SHAPED CURVE

After many observations of similar patterns of variation, mathematicians saw that variations followed a regular, symmetrical, bell shaped pattern. In Figure 3–2, a bell-shaped curve is superimposed over the measured points. The bell pattern is a distribution one would expect if there were no abnormal factors influencing the process. The bell shaped pattern is called the normal curve.

ABNORMAL VARIATION DISTORTS THE BELL SHAPE

Variation due to unnatural, abnormal factors distorts the bell curve. For example, measuring instruments that read high would move the distribution toward the top of the specification spread, as can be seen in Figure 3–3. The challenge is to

FIGURE 3–3
Abnormal Variation

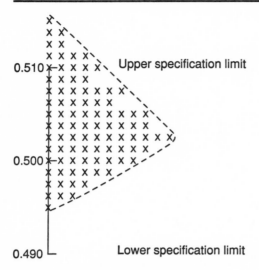

Specification spread is 0.500" ± 0.010"

determine whether process variation is due to normal or abnormal causes.

CAUSES OF VARIATION CAN BE ISOLATED AND IDENTIFIED

Variation is detected and controlled through statistical process control (SPC). This method, based on statistical principles, allows an operator to detect deviations in a measured value and then adjust the process back to the target dimension.

Using control charts as shown in Figure 3–4, the operator of a machine process can determine if the variation is normal or abnormal. These charts tell operators whether to intervene and remove abnormal causes or whether to leave the process alone.

THREE IMPORTANT QUESTIONS

The customer wants to know that a supplier is monitoring, controlling, and improving its critical processes. The problem is

FIGURE 3–4
Process in Control

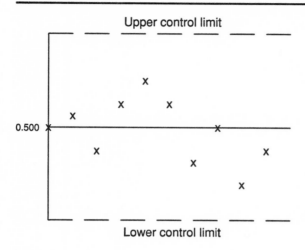

that a supplier can make products for years and pay little attention to improving the manufacturing process.

So, the customer should always ask the supplier the following questions:

- Are your major processes in control?
- Are your major processes capable?
- How will your processes be improved?

ARE YOUR MAJOR PROCESSES IN CONTROL?

A process in control, usually called statistical control, has its process measurements plotted inside calculated action limits on a variable control chart. If measured points are inside the control limits and follow a random pattern, variation in the process is natural, as shown in Figure 3–4. If the process is running naturally, the operator leaves the process alone.

OUT OF CONTROL

When a change in a process occurs, results can be seen on the variable control chart. So, if points follow a nonrandom pattern such as a rising trend or are outside the control limits, an

FIGURE 3–5
Process Out of Control

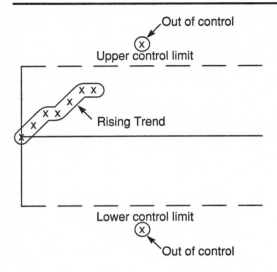

abnormal condition exists which should be immediately eliminated, as shown on Figure 3–5.

If the operator recognizes a nonrandom pattern of measurements or a point outside control limits, the operator identifies the cause, adjusts the process, and eliminates the immediate cause. The immediate cause of the unnatural variation may not be the root cause. Eliminating the root cause usually requires more time.

Out of control or abnormal conditions follow recognizable trends on the chart as shown in Figure 3–6. These trends are:

- Changes or jumps in level.
- Trends or steady changes in level.
- Recurring cycles.
- Two distinct populations.

To understand and identify the causes of the abnormal conditions, thorough knowledge of SPC is required. A complete analysis of SPC is beyond the scope of this book. Its value however, can be illustrated by an example of changes or jumps in a chart. For example, if there is a sudden change or jump in level on a variable chart, possible causes can be:

FIGURE 3–6
Out of Control Conditions

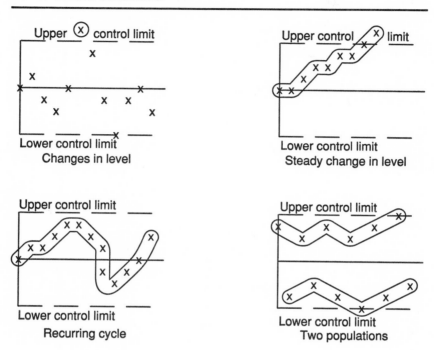

Changes in level

Steady change in level

Recurring cycle

Two populations

- The operator. A new or inexperienced operator may overadjust a process.
- The material. Raw material may vary in physical or chemical properties.
- The method. Procedures change between shifts.
- The machine. A machine has a new fixture or tooling that changes the basic settings.

IS THE PROCESS CAPABLE OF MEETING CUSTOMER SPECIFICATIONS?

Process capability is evaluated after abnormal causes have been identified, monitored, and eliminated, and the process is in statistical control. Then process spread can be compared with specification spread to determine whether specifications can be achieved and consistently met.

FIGURE 3–7
Cp = 1

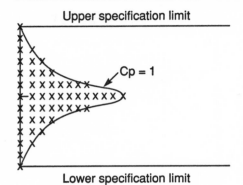

Upper specification limit

Cp = 1

Lower specification limit

Cp and Cpk are two common measures of capability. Both compare specification spread with process spread. Cpk, however, specifically measures how well centered the process spread is compared with the specification spread. It also measures the tightness of the variation spread.

If Cp equals 1 and the bell curve representing process spread is centered in the middle of the specification spread, then by definition the process has 99.7 percent of its products within the specification spread, as shown in Figure 3–7. This is, however, still 3,000 parts per million defectives, which is still unacceptable. If Cp = 2 and the bell curve is centered in the middle of the specification spread, then there are only 3.4 parts per million defectives. This leads us to the next question.

HOW WILL THE PROCESS BE IMPROVED?

To improve the process, variation around the specification target, the middle of the specification, has to be minimized. The capability index will increase, which means that the bell curve should be centered in the middle of the specification spread and is narrower, with a higher peak, as indicated in Figure 3–8. If this process of improvement continues, the bell curve becomes so narrow that the probability of a point appearing outside the specification limits is in the realm of parts-per-million (PPM).

FIGURE 3–8
Continuous Improvement

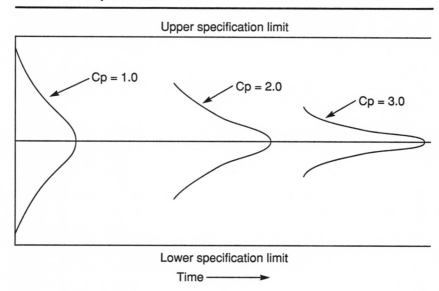

Upper specification limit

Cp = 1.0

Cp = 2.0

Cp = 3.0

Lower specification limit

Time ⟶

Often management action is required to improve a process once it is in statistical control. Management action means focusing on eliminating or minimizing the natural causes of variation, which is a significant conceptual contribution of W. Edwards Deming. Deming, an eminent quality authority, proposed that management controls 85 percent of the process while the operator only controls 15 percent of the improvement. For example, if a machine cannot consistently produce products that conform to a specification, management may have to authorize the purchase of a new machine. Another management option may be to relax the specifications.

DOES SPC WORK?

Much has been written about (SPC) being the panacea for all manufacturing ills. This may exaggerate the accomplishments of this prevention tool. Properly used, however, SPC can result in the following benefits:

- Provides objective and measurable feedback on supplier quality performance.
- Improves product flow.
- Pushes control of material quality on to the supplier.
- Eliminates sorting or incoming inspection.
- Improves product quality.
- Reduces need to accept off-standard parts.
- Reduces costs.
- Lowers scrap and rework.

SINGLE SOURCE PARTNERING

An inevitable result of the drive to continuous improvement is that products and services are eventually single sourced. Multiple sourcing tends to create complexity, which often results in a problem waiting to happen. It is much easier to work with one or a few suppliers than with many. Multiple suppliers can cause additional unwanted variation in performance, which shows up in poor communication, cooperation, and coordination. Such a situation results in overall poor quality. This has become a major justification for partnering.

NOTES

[1]This material was previously covered in Greg Hutchins, *Introduction to Quality: Management, Assurance and Control*, NY: Macmillan, 1990.

[2]Roy Williams, "Ambiguity Impedes Quality in the Service Industries," *Quality Progress*, July 1987, pp. 14–17.

[3]Kate Evans-Correia, "Adding Value to Floppy Disks," *Purchasing*, October 27, 1988, pp. 82–83.

[4]Charles Exley, "The Masterstroke of Managing for Stakeholders," *Directors & Boards*, Fall 1988, pp. 4–7.

[5]See David Garvin's Managing Quality, *The Free Press*, 1988, for an excellent discussion of the dimensions of quality.

[6]Miriam Cu-Uy-Gam, "Security Design Method Discussed," *Computing Canada*, October 18, 1984.

[7]Greg Hutchins, *Introduction to Quality: Management, Assurance, and Control*, NY: Macmillan, 1991.

Chapter Four

Continuous Supplier Improvement

This chapter traces the evolution of customer quality requirements, from inspecting a dimensional quality attribute in incoming material inspection, to requiring that suppliers apply for the Malcolm Baldrige National Quality Award. The evolution is depicted in Figure 4–1. The steps are not totally discrete because they flow into each other. However, the figure is useful for communicating the evolution of quality. The evolution of companywide, continuous improvement illustrates the accelerating trend towards integrating single-source supplier-partners into the customer's operations and into the product development cycle.

This chapter cannot exhaustively cover all types of customer-supplier continuous improvement efforts. Only the following major evolutionary milestones are discussed:

- Incoming material inspection.
- Quality systems.
- Statistical quality control.
- Companywide quality management.
- Malcolm Baldrige National Quality Award.

FIGURE 4–1
Ever-Higher Quality

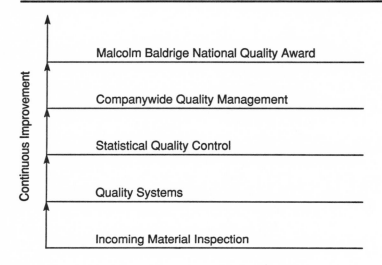

INCOMING MATERIAL INSPECTION

Inspection was once routinely used and in some cases is still used to determine the quality of material. At each step of production, from incoming, inprocess, to final product, products were inspected to determine their conformance to specifications. For example, in incoming material inspection, shipped products were inspected at the customer's receiving dock to determine whether they conformed to engineering specifications. If they conformed, they were accepted and sent to inventory or into production. If they did not conform, they were segregated and returned to the supplier for rework.

Incoming material inspection is based on a statistical sampling plan. The sampling plan tells the inspector that, given a number of products in a shipment and a desired quality level, a specified number of products is pulled from the shipment and inspected. Depending on the number of defective products in the sample, the shipment is either accepted or rejected. Sometimes another sample is pulled and inspected. Quality is usually measured in terms of defects-per-100 or 1,000 units. The major problem is that quality can't be improved through after-the-fact statistical sampling or 100 percent inspection.

SPECIAL PRODUCTS

One hundred percent inspection is still used for special products and in certain applications. One hundred percent inspection can check compliance with:

- Government regulations.
  The Food and Drug Administration (FDA) requires 100 percent sampling of certain products dealing with health or safety.
- Special requirements.
  Air safety requires 100 percent inspection of baggage.
- One of a kind products.
  NASA requires 100 percent testing and inspection of payloads going into space, because field repair is impossible or expensive.
- Very expensive products.
  Diamonds and products with high perceived quality are inspected.[1]

DISADVANTAGES OF INSPECTION

Regardless, inspection by humans, whether 100 percent or statistical sampling, has the following disadvantages:

- Wasteful.
  Sampling and inspection add cost and decrease value because products have to be moved; material can be damaged in handling, storage, or movement; each inspected part is measured and analyzed; space has to be allocated for inspection, inventory, and equipment; test and measurement equipment has to be purchased; personnel have to be trained; and the entire process requires time.

- Inaccurate.
  An inspector may become hypnotized by inspection and make mistakes. Even 100 percent inspection is only 80 percent effective because of the possibility of human errors.
- Impractical.
  Inspection of certain products is impractical because it may involve destructive testing.
- Wrong message.
  Inspection communicates to people and to suppliers that bad parts will still be accepted. There is no urgency for the supplier to improve quality.
- High risks.
  In sampling and inspection, there is a risk of accepting bad lots and rejecting good lots.
- No continuous improvement.
  Sampling is still inspection, not prevention, so that quality cannot be continuously improved.

QUALITY SYSTEMS

In 1959, the Department of Defense (DOD) issued a quality standard, MIL-Q 9858A, to ensure compliance with defense contracts (see Table 4–1). This became the highest level military quality standard. In the early 1960s, many military and commercial aerospace companies adopted this standard and developed internal quality programs based on it.

These quality programs emphasized internal systems and procedures to control product quality, specifically by:

- Performing incoming, in-process, and final material inspection.
- Monitoring manufacturing processes.
- Controlling supplied material.
- Calibrating measurement and test equipment.
- Developing womb-to-tomb documentation.

The assumption was that if the systems were in place, operating properly and documenting quality, quality could be controlled and ensured. This military standard served its purposes well, but

TABLE 4–1
MIL-Q-9858A

Quality Requirements

1. *Scope*
1.1 Applicability
1.2 Contractual Intent
1.3 Summary
1.4 Relation to Other Contract Requirements
1.5 Mil-I-45208

2. *Superseding, Supplementation, and Ordering*
2.1 Applicable Documents
2.2 Amendments and Revisions
2.3 Ordering Government Documents

3. *Quality Program Management*
3.1 Organization
3.2 Initial Quality Planning
3.3 Work Instructions
3.4 Records
3.5 Corrective Action
3.6 Costs Related to Quality

4. *Facilities and Standards*
4.1 Drawings, Documentation, and Changes
4.2 Measuring and Testing Equipment
4.3 Production Tooling
4.4 Use of Contractor's Inspection Equipment
4.5 Advanced Metrology Requirements

5. *Control of Purchases*
5.1 Responsibility
5.2 Purchasing Data

6. *Manufacturing Control*
6.1 Materials and Materials Control
6.2 Production Processing and Fabrication
6.3 Completed Item
6.4 Handling, Storage, and Delivery
6.5 Nonconforming Material
6.6 Statistical Quality Control and Analysis
6.7 Indication and Inspection Status

7. *Coordinated Government/Contractor Actions*
7.1 Government Inspection at Subcontractor or Vendor Facilities
7.2 Government Property

8. *Notes*
8.1 Intended Use
8.2 Exemptions

in a competitive global economy it has problems. The standard does not emphasize or address final customer satisfaction, internal customer satisfaction, strategic quality, quality planning, prevention, or continuous improvement. SPC or other statistical techniques are mentioned, but are not stressed. Engineering and other company related quality areas are glossed over. Another problem is that there are no specific quality targets or benchmarks that suppliers must achieve. Furthermore, documentation requirements are so extensive that cynics contend quality is being papered over rather than progressively improved.

The Department of Defense (DOD) still requires contractors to comply with this or with less-stringent quality standards. Realizing that the U.S. military procurement structure is in a state of flux, DOD is trying to wean military contractors away from the guaranteed margins of military contracting to more commercial, market-driven quality emphasizing prevention through statistically driven continuous improvement.

STATISTICAL QUALITY CONTROL

The first commercial improvement efforts focused on the control of quality during production. It was generally acknowledged that quality could not be improved through after the fact inspection. It was decided that the process that made the product, either internally or externally, should be monitored and controlled through statistically driven prevention techniques, specifically statistical process control. Both product manufacturers and service providers are now encouraged to use statistical techniques. This stage is considered a major jump for suppliers because it stresses measurable, attainable continuous improvement.

In this stage, customers specify quality levels, testing methods, and internal controls. For example, capability indices specify required quality levels. Testing methods include: first item inspection, failure mode and effects analysis (FMEA), and reliability testing. Internal control systems emphasize quality plans, supplied approved materials, system audits, process controls, and engineering design controls.

Quality is defined in terms of conformance to specifications and in terms of the customer's perspective, specifically satisfying the entire range of the final customer's wants and needs. Quality is also pushed upstream into engineering and manufacturing-engineering. Customers evaluate suppliers in terms of overall value, which is an optimum blend of quality, price, technology, and delivery.

By using a defect prevention technique such as statistical process control (SPC), parts per million (PPM) quality levels can conceivably be attained. This quality level is now required for a preferred (ship to assembly) supplier, as far as many automotive and electronic companies are concerned.

FORD MOTOR COMPANY'S QUALITY EFFORT

Ford Motor Company was one of the first U.S. companies to adopt statistically driven improvement efforts, both internally and among suppliers. To be more competitive in the emerging world marketplace, Ford revamped its purchasing and inventory practices in 1979 and developed plans to involve suppliers more closely and earlier in its product planning, design, and production cycles. SPC was a cornerstone of this effort.

In March 1983, Ford announced that SPC programs would be phased into the overall quality rating of suppliers. Three months later, Ford invited suppliers to send plant, quality control, and production managers to a six-hour training seminar on SPC. By October 1984, Ford expected its suppliers to implement SPC programs at their plant manufacturing locations. The suppliers who met the stringent quality requirements gained preferential treatment in new part development and a preferred position in source selection.[2]

The guiding principles behind Ford's quality system standard illuminate the importance that Ford and many other organizations give to quality and continuous improvement:[3]

- Quality comes first - To achieve customer satisfaction, the quality of our products and services must be our number one priority.

- Customers are the focus of everything we do - Our work must be done with our customers in mind, providing better products and services than our competition.
- Continuous improvement is essential to our success - We must strive for excellence in everything we do: in our products, in their safety and value - and in our services, our human relations, our competitiveness, and our profitability.
- Employee involvement is our way of life - We are a team. We must treat each other with trust and respect.
- Dealers and suppliers are our partners - The Company must maintain mutually beneficial relationships with dealers, suppliers, and our other business associates.
- Integrity is never compromised - The conduct of our Company worldwide must be pursued in a manner that is socially responsible and commands respect for its integrity and for its positive contributions to society. Our doors are open to men and women alike without discrimination and without regard to ethnic origin or personal beliefs.

Following an audit, a candidate supplier is awarded a score on criteria spelled out in the quality standard. This determines the supplier's status, which in the certification process can range from candidate to preferred. Suppliers falling within certain ranges continue to get business, contingent upon further improvement. If the score is sufficiently high, the supplier becomes a supplier-partner. Suppliers below a certain level are asked to work with the customer to improve quickly or start losing business. You can get a feeling for the scope of the standard by referring to Table 4–2.

CONTINUOUS IMPROVEMENT

Ford Motor Company initially established its quality standard, Q-101, for its first tier suppliers. Now Ford's first tier suppliers are mandating that their suppliers comply with the same stringent criteria. In one case, a fourth-tier supplier to Ford, a small-

TABLE 4–2
Q-101 Table of Contents

1. *Introduction*
1.1 Ford Motor Company's Quality Expectations
1.2 Quality System Evidence Requirements
1.3 How to Use This Document

2. *Planning for Quality*
2.1 Process Flow Chart
2.2 Feasibility
2.3 Failure Mode and Effects Analysis (FMEA)
2.4 Control Plans
2.5 Gage Planning
2.6 Preliminary Process Capability
2.7 Process Monitoring and Control Instructions
2.8 Packaging Planning
2.9 Initial Sample Approval Requirements
2.10 Prototype Part Quality Initiatives
2.11 Incoming Raw Material and Parts Control
2.12 Planning for Ongoing Quality

3. *Achieving Process and Product Quality*
3.1 Ongoing Process Capability
3.2 Statistical Process Control (SPC)
3.3 Product Qualification and Monitoring
3.4 Measuring and Test Equipment
3.5 Engineering Specification (ES) Test Performance Requirements
3.6 Indication of Product Status
3.7 Verification of New Set-ups
3.8 Reference Samples
3.9 Reworked Products
3.10 Returned Product Analysis
3.11 Problem Solving Methods
3.12 Scheduled Preventive Maintenance
3.13 Heat-Treated Parts
3.14 Lot Traceability
3.15 Continuous Improvement

4. *Documenting Quality*
4.1 Procedures
4.2 Records
4.3 Drawings and Change Control
4.4 Part/Process Modification Control
4.5 Changes in Manufacturing Processes

5. *Special Requirements for Control Item Products*
5.1 Quality Planning
5.2 Documentation

6. *System and Initial Sample Approvals*
6.1 Requirements for New Products
6.2 Plant Quality Surveys
6.3 Review and Approval of Initial Samples

Reprinted with permission from the "Ford Worldwide Quality System Q-101," by Ford Motor Company, 1990.

job shop, has had to satisfy the same criteria as the first tier, billion-dollar supplier.

The purpose of this and similar quality standards is to elevate the quality, performance, and technology of the entire supplier base. As more suppliers reach the preferred status—in Ford's case, it is called Q1—a new quality level is established that suppliers must achieve.

In the early 1990s, as most of Ford's suppliers are certified to the Q1 level, the next step in the continuous improvement journey is Ford's Total Quality Excellence, which is discussed next.

COMPANYWIDE QUALITY MANAGEMENT

At this stage, the supplier becomes more integrated into the customer's organization, in product development and in the communication chain. Once a product is introduced into the marketplace, the supplier is involved in continuously updating and enhancing the product through the product lifecycle. This does not necessarily mean the supplier loses its autonomy—just that the supplier is encouraged to have many of the attributes of the best organizations in its particular industry. In other words, it must be world-class.

This stage of continuous improvement goes by several names. At Ford Motor Company, it is called Total Quality Excellence. The ISO 9000, a set of European quality standards, refers to it as Companywide Quality Management. Some organizations call it Total Quality Control or Total Quality Management. Regardless of its name, continuous improvement is integrated company and supplierwide into marketing, design engineering, manufacturing engineering, production, purchasing, distribution, and service areas.

Quality is no longer defined as simply meeting specifications and customer requirements, but includes satisfying and exceeding customer wants, needs, and expectations in the product and service quality related areas discussed in the previous chapter. In this stage, customer satisfaction and continuous improvement are emphasized in all elements of the organization and supplier base. It includes elements of total quality excellence, supplier certification, benchmarking, quality function deployment, Just-In-Time, manufacturer-supplier partnerships, total customer service, automation, design excellence, and value analysis. The goal is to achieve total continuous improvement throughout the supplier's operations.

TOTAL QUALITY EXCELLENCE

Ford Motor Company's Total Quality Excellence is based on self certification. A supplier first appraises its operations to determine its level of compliance. If the supplier believes the conditions of the standard are being satisfied, then the supplier asks the customer for an on-site evaluation. A multidisciplinary customer team then audits the supplier and assigns a score. Score totals are shown on the standard. (see Table 4–3)

TQE Award is broader than Ford's Q1 Preferred Quality Award. The Q1 award is awarded for quality excellence. The purpose of the Total Quality Excellence Award is to recognize a high level of excellence and overall continuous improvement. This is required if "Ford Motor Company's vision is to be a low-cost producer of the highest quality products and services which provide the best customer value."[4] To achieve this goal, TQE is only awarded to Ford's best Q1 suppliers.

TQE is based on many of the principles we have been discussing throughout this book. Specifically, TQE principles involve the following:

- Quality is defined by the customer.
- Quality excellence is best achieved by preventing problems from occurring.
- All work done by company employees, suppliers, and dealers is part of a process that creates a product or service for a customer.
- Sustained quality excellence requires continuous process improvement.
- People provide the intelligence and generate the actions necessary to realize these improvements.
- Each employee is a customer for work done by other employees or suppliers.[5]

TABLE 4–3
Ford Motor Company's Total Quality Excellence Criteria

Functional Area	Total Points Possible	Functional Area	Total Points Possible
Engineering:			
Product Design		*Processing*	
Design Engineering	3	All components	
Sales Engineers	1	manufactured starting	
System Design	3	with base raw material	3
Component Design	4		
FMEA	3	Material and/or	
Manufacturing Feasibility	2	component suppliers	
Computer Aided Design	2	provide statistical	
FEA or Other Modeling	2	control data.	3
Subtotal	20		
Development		All process contained at	
Development Engineering	4	surveyed locations	3
Product Development	3		
Material Development	3	Process control points	
R&D Laboratory	2	clearly defined	2
Prototype Build	5		
Prototype Tooling Build	2	Statistical control methods	
Other	1	used within the process	4
Subtotal	20	Subtotal	15
Product Test		*Manufacturing Support*	
Test Equipment	3		
Durability Testing	4	Productive Maintenance	
Engineering Specification	3	Program:	
Product	3		
Material	2	Control System Scheduled	
Subtotal	15	Maintenance	1
		Spare Parts Control	1
Manufacturing Engineering		Tool/Machine Rehab	1
Manufacturing Engineering	3	Tool/Die/Mold/Gage	
Process Engineering	2	Design	3
Industrial Engineering	1	Tool Room	3
Process FMEA	2	Layout Inspection	2
Manufacturing Feasibility	3	Machine Shop	1
Process Sheets	2	Machine Design	1
Production Sign-Off	2	Tool/Die/Mold Build	2
Subtotal	15	Subtotal	15
		Total rating points	100

TABLE 4–3
Continued

Description	Total Points Possible
Delivery	
• Utilization of the Ford Motor Company Supplier Communications System.	25
• Shipment performance in relation to 3086 release quantities and ship date requirements.	25
• Overall supplier performance (ie. suggests improvements, supports Ford Motor Co. programs such as JIT, etc.).	17
• Timely supplier response to problems.	13
• Frequency of over-shipments.	10
• Timely reconciliation of cumulative shipments.	5
• Frequency and dollar volume of premium freight charges.	5
Total rating points	100
Commercial:	
I. Worldwide Cost Competitiveness	
1. First Year Cost (annualized piece price plus tool cost)	15
2. Ongoing Productivity Commitment	15
3. Engineering Change Costs	5
4. Cost Savings Contributions	5
Subtotal	40
II. Capability	
1. Management Depth	8
2. Financial Resources	7
3. Manufacturing Flexibility	5
4. Manufacturing Technology	5
Subtotal	25
III. Responsiveness to Business Issues	
1. Quotations (timeliness and thoroughness, including feasibility assessments)	8
2. New Part Launch Performance (meets sample promise dates, supports timing and quantities)	13
3. Adaptability to Changing Environment (long-term contracts, JIT, SPC, CAD/CAM, etc.)	6
4. Responsiveness to Buyer in Problem Solving Situations (quality, delivery, strike protection, service to Ford Motor Co. plant, etc.) and on Day-to-Day business issues.	8
Subtotal	35
Total rating points	100

Reprinted with permission from the "Total Quality Excellence Program" by Ford Motor Company, 1989, p. 8.

WORLD CLASS SUPPLIERS

At this level, customers are directly dependent on the performance of their suppliers to maintain and improve quality at a competitive cost. The best suppliers become an extension of the manufacturer-customer in terms of having similar management policies, structure, information systems, quality levels, delivery schedules, and costing practices.

The goal is to form integrated business partnerships with world-class suppliers so that products and services are kept competitive. To do this, key supplier-partners simultaneously develop and engineer parts for the next generation of products.

MALCOLM BALDRIGE NATIONAL QUALITY AWARD

The Malcolm Baldrige National Quality Award is the U.S. equivalent of the Japanese Deming Prize. The award is given to small business, manufacturing, and service companies. The annual award recognizes U.S. companies that excel in quality achievement and quality management. Recent winners include: Westinghouse, Motorola, Xerox Corporation, Milliken, an IBM division, the Cadillac division of GM, Federal Express, Wallace Company, and Globe Metallurgical. The award promotes:

- Awareness of quality as an important element of competitiveness.
- Understanding the requirements for quality excellence.
- Sharing information on successful quality strategies and on the benefits derived from implementation of these strategies.

Candidates submit applications that assess internal quality (assessment criteria are shown in Table 4–4. Applicants provide information and data on their quality processes, progress in quality improvement, and customer orientation.

TABLE 4–4
Malcolm Baldrige National Quality Award Assessment Criteria
Examination Categories/Items

	Maximum Points
1.0 *Leadership*	100

The Leadership category examines how senior executives create and sustain clear and visible quality values, along with a management system, to guide all activities of the company toward quality excellence. Also examined are the senior executives' and the company's quality leadership in the external community, and how the company integrates its public responsibilities with its quality values and practices.

1.1 Senior Executive Leadership	40
1.2 Quality Values	15
1.3 Management for Quality	25
1.4 Public Responsibility	20

2.0 *Information and Analysis*	70

The Information and Analysis category examines the scope, validity, use, and management of data and information that underlie the company's overall quality management system. Also examined is the adequacy of the data, information, and analysis to support a responsive prevention-based approach to quality and customer satisfaction based upon "management by fact."

2.1 Scope and Management of Quality Data and Information	20
2.2 Competitive Comparisons and Benchmarks	30
2.3 Analysis of Quality Data and Information	20

3.0 *Strategic Quality Planning*	60

The Strategic Quality Planning category examines the company's planning process for achieving or retaining quality leadership, and how the company integrates quality improvement planning into overall business planning. Also examined are the company's short-term and longer-term priorities to achieve and/or sustain a quality leadership position.

3.1 Strategic Quality Planning Process	35
3.2 Quality Goals and Plans	25

4.0 *Human Resource Utilization*	150

The Human Resource Utilization category examines the effectiveness of the company's efforts to develop and realize the full potential of the work force, including management, and to maintain an environment conducive to full participation, quality leadership, and personal and organizational growth.

4.1 Human Resource Management	20
4.2 Employee Involvement	40
4.3 Quality Education and Training	40
4.4 Employee Recognition and Performance Measurement	25
4.5 Employee Well Being and Morale	25

TABLE 4–4
Continued

	Maximum Points
5.0 *Quality Assurance of Products and Services*	140

The Quality Assurance of Products and Services category examines the systematic approaches used by the company for assuring quality of goods based primarily upon process design and control, including control of procured materials, parts, and services. Also examined is the integration of process control with continuous quality improvement.

5.1 Design and Introduction of Quality Products and Services	35
5.2 Process Quality Control	20
5.3 Continuous Improvement of Processes	20
5.4 Quality Assessment	15
5.5 Documentation	10
5.6 Business Process and Support Service Quality	20
5.7 Supplier Quality	20

6.0 *Quality Results*	180

The Quality Results category examines quality levels and quality improvement based upon objective measures derived from analysis of customer requirements and expectations, and from analysis of business operations. Also examined are current quality levels in relation to those of competing firms.

6.1 Product and Service Quality Results	90
6.2 Business Process, Operational, and Support Service Quality Results	50
6.3 Supplier Quality Results	40

7.0 *Customer Satisfaction*	300

The Customer Satisfaction category examines the company's knowledge of the customer, overall customer service systems, responsiveness, and its ability to meet requirements and expectations. Also examined are current levels and trends in customer satisfaction.

7.1 Determining Customer Requirements and Expectations	30
7.2 Customer Relationship Management	50
7.3 Customer Service Standards	20
7.4 Commitment to Customers	15
7.5 Complaint Resolution for Quality Improvement	25
7.6 Determining Customer Satisfaction	20
7.7 Customer Satisfaction Results	70
7.8 Customer Satisfaction Comparison	70
Total Points	<u>1000</u>

Source: 1991 Application Guidelines—Malcolm Baldrige National Quality Award.

AWARD SELECTION PROCESS

At this level, quality is mainly defined in terms of customer satisfaction, which is 30 percent of the award. This stage of quality assumes that if quality management systems are in place and are integrated throughout the organization, including the supplier base, the results will be quality products and services that exceed customer expectations.

The National Quality Award is managed by NIST, the National Institute of Standards and Technology. The quality award has only existed for several years but has gained in popularity. Many companies are applying and are requiring their suppliers to apply for the award.

The award follows a similar application review procedure as Ford's TQE award. The specifics of the procedure are as follows:

- Application completed.
  Applicant fills out a self assessment, application form.
- First stage review.
  A board of examiners reviews the application to determine if minimum criteria have been met. If they have, the application is forwarded to the next step.
- Consensus review.
  A group of examiners reviews the applications and a consensus of the examiner's identifies the applications that should be sent to the panel of judges. The judges consider applications on a case-by-case basis, review the scoring by the board of examiners, and review the scoring profiles in each award category: manufacturing, service, and small business.
- Site visit review.
  The highest scoring candidates for the award are visited by the examining board. The objectives of the site visits are to verify the information on the application form and to clarify issues and questions raised during the review of the application.
- Judges final review.
  A final review of all evaluation reports is conducted by the panel of judges who then make a recommendation of whom should receive the award.

PLEASE APPLY FOR THE AWARD!

Organizations recognize that their competitiveness depends on their supplier-partners. Therefore, many companies are now evaluating and auditing their suppliers based on the national quality award criteria. Any supplier that does not is usually disqualified. Recently Motorola, a 1988 award winner, informed its suppliers they must compete for the award.

Is this an isolated occurrence? No. More and more companies, manufacturing, research and development, service, and government organizations, are encouraging and often mandating higher quality levels, lowered costs, improved service, and enhanced technology from suppliers.

The government, particularly the Department of Defense, is encouraging contractors to develop Total Quality Management (TQM) systems in order to ease the transition from military contracts to commercial product development. And then there are companies, like Motorola, that urge suppliers to aim for the National Quality Award. Motorola was one of the first and most visible companies to require pursuit of these world-class quality standards.

Sometimes an organization's motive for applying for the award is suspect. The motive is based more on garnering visibility and recognition than it is on improving systems and becoming competitive.

INTERNATIONAL QUALITY

Time consuming and costly supplier quality rating systems once proliferated throughout Europe. Companies in different countries evaluated their suppliers' quality processes and products based on their own particular specifications. Likewise, companies within an industry evaluated the same suppliers against similar specifications. These rating systems only created confusion and redundancy.

If all goes as planned, by the end of 1992 the European Community (EC) will become a single integrated market, free of most trade barriers among its 12 members. So that products are freely traded, EC has been harmonizing standards, including those dealing with quality management and assurance systems.

European governments and companies want assurance that products produced by EC member and non-EC member nations comply with recognized quality requirements. Requirements were eventually developed that evolved into the ISO (International Organization for Standardization) 9000 series quality standards. ISO's goal is to promote the development of worldwide standards among its 91 members which in the United States is represented by the American National Standards Institute (ANSI).

ISO 9000

Companies that operate in Europe are widely adopting the ISO 9000 series to document and demonstrate their quality systems. It is generally believed that after 1992 every contract and specification written by European companies and governments will require a supplier to demonstrate compliance to one of the ISO quality standards. To accomplish this, the EC nations have, or are establishing, third party registration and government-sponsored accrediting councils to evaluate suppliers' quality systems. The major benefit is that once a supplier is registered, it does not have to be audited by all of its customers.

The ISO 9000 series is a set of five separate but related international quality management and assurance standards. The series of standards outline the requirements for a quality management system. The five standards in the series are:

- ISO 9000—Quality management and quality assurance standards—Guidelines for selection and use.
- ISO 9001—Quality systems—Model for quality assurance in design and development, production, installation, and servicing.
- ISO 9002—Quality systems—Model for quality assurance in production and installation.

- ISO 9003—Model for quality assurance in final inspection and test.
- ISO 9004—Quality management and quality system guidelines.

ISO 9000 guides the user in selecting ISO 9001, 9002, 9003 and 9004. ISO 9001, 9002, and 9003 are quality system models for evaluating suppliers. ISO 9004 is used primarily for assessing internal quality management systems. ISO 9004 identifies quality responsibilities in different organizational areas from marketing and market research to final disposal of the product. The major elements of ISO 9004 are discussed in Table 4.5.

REGISTRATION

Commonly, European companies are expecting U.S. suppliers to have their quality systems registered to ISO 9001, 9002, or 9003. An accredited, independent, third party first conducts an on-site audit of a supplier's operations using the appropriate quality standard. If the assessment shows deficiencies, the supplier is expected to correct them.

Once corrected, the supplier is issued a registration certificate stating that its quality systems comply with the appropriate ISO standard. The supplier is then listed in a public register maintained by the third party registration organization.

The benefits of registration include:

- Wide recognition and acceptance of the standard.
- Avoiding duplication of audits.
- Access to markets (such as EC).
- Use of the registration logo in marketing and advertising.
- Improved quality and reduced costs.

Registration is not life long. Periodically, the third party registrar will conduct a partial assessment to ensure that the supplier's quality systems are being maintained. As well, every three or four years the registrar will conduct a full audit to

TABLE 4-5
Elements of ANSI/ASQC-Q94 (ISO—9004)

● *Marketing and Market Research*
Marketing is responsible for distilling customer needs, wants, and requirements, and communicating these to the organization. Marketing identifies a market, identifies customer requirements, develops a product brief, and establishes a feedback system between customer and organization. The market may be an entirely new market, an established market, or a niche of an established market. The important point is that the marketplace is changing and marketing must have a good sense of the specific wants, needs, and expectations of customers in different niches. This information will be used to design, produce, and deliver a product that satisfies the customer.

● *Design/Specification Engineering*
Engineering translates customer requirements into technical specifications for materials, products, and processes. The product design must satisfy customer requirements, but also optimize cost, manufacturability, safety, government regulations, testability, and design quality. Engineering must assign responsibilities and establish timelines so that a reliable product can be produced. Especially with complex products involving different disciplines, checkpoints are established throughout the development process so multidisciplinary teams can evaluate and review the design. If changes are necessary, they can be incorporated easily. The product should be manufacturable and testable. As the product is being manufactured, the methods, personnel, and test equipment should be spelled out.

● *Purchasing*
Purchasing is responsible for distilling internal wants, needs, and expectations of the organization, and communicating these to suppliers. Purchasing is responsible for managing the supplier throughout the product life cycle, including selecting, evaluating, monitoring, and improving suppliers. The supplier must understand what is expected in terms of quality, delivery, and service. Purchasing must then assemble and transmit the information so that the supplier knows what is expected. At a minimum, purchasing communicates requirements to suppliers, including: quality specifications, service characteristics, operating environment, aesthetics, quality grade, inspection instructions, process quality requirements, and product specifications.

● *Production*
Production is responsible for creating reality out of engineering specifications and drawings. Production is a loose term that includes assembly, fabrication, and if required, on-line inspection. As discussed earlier, quality is the study of variation. The secret to achieving quality is to define each step in the production process and limit any variation at the specification target. Therefore all critical production elements must be controlled if quality is to be ensured. This means that each production step is defined and controlled. Incoming raw material has uniform characteristics. Operators have been trained in the use of the machines. The methods used by the operators are the same. The machines are also capable of producing products to specifications.

TABLE 4–5
Continued

- *Inspection, Test, and Examination*
  Quality is only as good as the accuracy and precision of measuring instruments. The process engineer or operator must be confident that the decisions based on the measurement data are reliable. As specifications become tighter, test equipment must measure parts accurately. Measurement and test equipment must be calibrated periodically, so they provide repeatable measurements. The level of testing depends on the process, risk to the consumer, risk to the producer, cost, and regulations.
- *Handling, Packaging, and Storage*
  Quality can only be maintained if products are packaged, stored, handled, and transported properly. Proper packaging storage, handling, and transport protects contents against heat, corrosion, temperature, and vibration.
- *Sales and Distribution*
  Once a product is sold, it must be delivered to the customer intact and in an expedient and courteous manner. If a product is damaged in transit or if another problem arises, the problem must be handled effectively and efficiently.
- *Installation and Operation*
  Complex industrial products may require specialized tools, equipment, methods or trained personnel to install and to operate. For example, complex equipment must have extensive manuals that describe safe installation and operation.
- *Technical Assistance and Maintenance*
  Once a product is sold, the buyer may require technical assistance to maintain its operation. Technical assistance may be nothing more than answering phone questions. Or, it may mean sending a trained technician to repair, replace, or maintain a sophisticated piece of equipment.
- *Disposal After Use*
  After use, a product has to be disposed properly and safely. If the product does not have any useful life, it is scrapped. Many products have their lives extended through preventive maintenance and repair. If a product is scrapped, it is done in such a way that it does not jeopardize safety, health, or environment.

---

determine continued compliance. If the supplier fails the audit, it must correct its quality systems or lose registration.

An important point of this chapter is the need for closer communication and integration through partnering between the customer and key suppliers, which is discussed next.

NOTES

[1]G. Hutchins, *Quality: The Competitive Edge*, Portland: QPE, 1988.

[2]James Lorincz, "Job 1 is Being Done with Statistical Process Control," *Purchasing World*, September 1985, pp. 34–38.

[3]Ford Motor Company, "Quality System Standards Q-101," 1990.

[4]Ford Motor Company, "Total Quality Excellence Program," 1989, p. 8.

[5]Ford pamphlet, "Ford Total Quality Excellence Award," 1989.

Chapter Five

Supplier Partnering

To attain the goal of global competitiveness and the objective of total customer satisfaction, a progressive partnering philosophy is evolving based on participatory problem solving, simultaneous product development, and integration of mutual capabilities to satisfy the final customer.

SCIENTIFIC MANAGEMENT

Frederick Taylor, the father of scientific management studied how workers worked and how supervisors supervised in the early part of this century. He developed a set of principles that were used for many years to manage work. Workers were told what to do, when to do it, and how to do it. This authoritarian style was a cutting edge philosophy in its time. It reflected the organizational environment of the early part of this century when factory work was mechanistic. Products did not change much and workers were looked upon as machines.

For years, Taylor's scientific management model was a fixture in the workplace, especially in small factories and job shops.

Much of industrial engineering is still mired in this mentality of time-motion, product costing, and machine capacity studies.

And this attitude still prevails in many organizations in the way work is parceled out to suppliers. A product is broken down into its basic elements. Everything is spelled out in detailed drawings, standards, and specifications. Even the right way to manufacture a product is often detailed on drawings. Suppliers do the work they are contracted to do. The buyer assumes that suppliers do not want to contribute to product improvement or are not equipped to do so. Also, work is divided among multiple suppliers to keep costs and curtailment risks low.

However, the nature of manufacturing and design work has changed dramatically in the last 20 years. The marketplace is fickle. Products change quickly. Product life cycles are cut in half. Work is no longer mechanistic and many machines are computerized. Production processes are tightly controlled to minimize variation. Tolerances are much tighter. Young workers are more willing to work and are more adaptable to change. Senior workers want to upgrade existing skills to achieve specific process expertise. And in the make or buy decision, more products are being bought from single source, worldclass supplier-partners.

PARTICIPATORY SOURCING

In many business relationships, the authoritarian style is being replaced by a more participatory style based on partnering. The authoritarian style assumed that employees (suppliers) must be controlled, directed, and punished if work was not properly performed. It also assumed that the average employee (supplier) was not responsible and did not want to improve. The authoritarian style of supplier management was based on the assumption that the customer knew everything about how a supplied product was to be designed and built. In this model, customer's management directed how supplied products would be produced. Suppliers were contracted to perform work with little or no input into product planning and development.

This is being replaced by the assumption that suppliers develop attitudes about their work based upon their ability to contribute. And the best way to induce suppliers to continuously improve is not through an authoritarian management style but through involvement, stressing open communication, trust building, and integrating skills. Internal product-development teams design and follow a product from conception to market introduction. Quality improvement teams solve workplace problems. Supplier teams work with the customer to design breakthrough products.

The participatory style has been embraced slowly in the manufacturing environment, whether in manufacturing engineering, purchasing, or design engineering. There are several reasons for this. These disciplines were considered professional. It was assumed that each professional could do his or her assigned tasks without direction or help from others.

Also, factory work was considered a remnant of the rustbelt mentality of doing business. Service was where cutting-edge management changes were occurring and the manufacturing environment was not pressured to adapt. As well, small suppliers—shops of 40 people or less—were started by entrepreneurs who tended to resist novel management philosophies.

PARTNERING

The partnering process evolved from the authoritarian and was originally driven by the need to maintain and improve product and service quality. The pursuit of quality, and then continuous improvement, became the holy grail of every company wanting to improve its financial condition. With a high percentage of the manufacturing dollar being outsourced, as well as much technology content being derived from suppliers, companies started to assess the capabilities of their supplier base. Basic assumptions were examined, such as the value of using multiple sources to keep prices low.

SINGLE VERSUS MULTIPLE SOURCING

Traditionally, purchasing stressed front-end price to select multiple suppliers for a product line. Then, purchasing offered various inducements to reward acceptable behavior and punishments to deter unacceptable behavior. This was an authoritarian approach to supplier management. The orientation was also based on a short-term and carrot-stick approach to business.

In previous years, multiple suppliers usually provided similar products. These suppliers competed yearly for the lion's share of the business, usually through lower pricing. The purchaser believed that multiple suppliers kept prices low, maintained supplier competition, and provided a safety valve if a major supplier could not deliver products because of an unforeseen event, such as a strike or fire.

There were risks however, in multiple sourcing. Suppliers may have kept prices low, but were not likely to improve product quality or service, which are requisites in a competitive economy. Suppliers were not motivated to adapt their operations to satisfy such customer needs as delivering just-in-time, containing costs, or enhancing service. In general, multiple sourcing resulted in:

- Variations in quality.
- Higher overall costs.
- Poor delivery.
- Increased purchasing time.
- Increased travel costs to visit supplier facilities.
- Loss of volume discounts.
- Spread confidential information.
- Increased investment in equipment.
- Increased investment in training.[1]

After evaluating the above risks, companies determined that the preferred option in many cases was to screen suppliers so that all the business for a product line or commodity went to a single supplier-partner.

Single sourcing is no panacea. There are risks. A supplier may not continuously improve. An unforeseen event, such as an act of God, may occur, which shuts the supplier's plant. To minimize exposure to risks, a single source is periodically audited to ensure that customer expectations have been heard and implemented. Also, a single source may be expected to have multiple plants or parallel machinery capable of manufacturing the same product.

Another option is to give the lion's share of the business to a main supplier and the rest to an acceptable alternate. For example, one supplier receives 80 percent of the business and an acceptable alternate receives 20 percent. At the end of the year, each supplier's performance is measured based on quality, price, availability, and service, and the percentages may change accordingly. In this way, both suppliers are motivated to continuously improve.

INTEGRATING SUPPLIERS

In a long-term partnership, a supplier is fully integrated into the customer's operations. The supplier is privy to the customer's strategies, including advanced product information, designs, and delivery requirements. The customer has access to the worldclass supplier's proprietary technology, manufacturing facilities, or unique capabilities.

Innovation and continuous improvement are accelerating so rapidly and becoming so specialized that companies cannot keep up. A common challenge is that a company may have a great idea but does not possess the physical resources to commercialize it. Following the principle that one does what one does best, contracting design and manufacturing to a partner is a common method for companies to gain access to resources quickly and economically.

Suppliers may be given a performance specification and asked to design, manufacture, and test a product that complies with the specification. This type of *black box* engineering necessarily results in a close working relationship between the customer and supplier. The customer benefits by lowering internal direct costs, reducing development costs, having access to proprietary technologies, spreading overhead costs, and having the ability to focus on areas in which it is expert.[2]

Suppliers of specialized products, such as chemicals and integrated circuits, are often logical candidates for partnering because they provide much needed design and quality information early in product development. By definition if they are worldclass, they should know more of the capabilities of the supplied part than the customer team designing the product. Over time, suppliers gain product knowledge and experience. The customer gains a long-term supply of competitively priced, quality parts.

Suppliers are asked to think for themselves when asked to design a particular part. In many cases, a supplier-partner simultaneously designs parts as the customer is developing a product. Suppliers may be asked to contribute a higher level of expertise, and to design and produce subassembly and assembly level products instead of just piece parts and components. Prototype prints handed to suppliers may spell out an application, but are vague in specifics. This is a long way from the prescription found in many older prints that said "build to print."

Partnering also simplifies problem solving. One supplier may be responsible for an entire assembly or system. Thus if a problem develops, responsibility can be pinpointed and the problem quickly resolved. For example, a dozen suppliers previously may have provided metal, mechanical and electrical components for an automotive assembly. If there was a problem, all of the component suppliers may have had to be contacted to determine responsibility and find a solution. With one supplier responsible for the entire assembly, corrective action is swift.

Profile of a Typical Partnership

The following example illustrates a partnering relationship. Most industrial gas suppliers provide generic products or services to their customers, which usually means delivering gases to the shipping dock of the semiconductor plant. In one partnering arrangement, Air Products and Chemicals contracted with Motorola to manage all the industrial gas functions at one facility for 10 years.

As an integrated Motorola supplier, Air Products supplies a full range of industrial and specialty gases, equipment, and technical services to Motorola, specifically agreeing to:

1. Design, specify, and install all the components for gas storage, safety, analysis, piping and monitoring systems.
2. Supply all gases, storage tanks, in-plant piping, purifiers, cabinets, and computerized monitoring of gases.
3. Maintain point of use purities.
4. Assign an on-site technical manager.[3]

Should all supplier-partners be integrated into the development team? No. Integration requires time and exposes more people to proprietary information that may provide a competitor with a market edge. Only suppliers that can add specific value should be integrated. Value may be a unique technology, distribution channels, capable processes, or proprietary products. Common sense should dictate this decision. It probably would make no sense to integrate an ordinary commodity supplier.

MANUFACTURER/DISTRIBUTOR PARTNERSHIPS

The partnership arrangement also extends to the distributor. At its simplest level, the distributor stocks a manufacturer's goods in exchange for a commitment to purchase a line of goods at specific margins for a period of time. Specifically, the customer commits to buy all of his/her MRO (maintenance, repair, and operating) products from the distributor, who promises to sell the goods at predetermined prices and to make certain they are available when a customer calls for them.[4] Distributors also may provide the customer with service, assortment, financial assistance, advice, and technical support.

Distributor-customer relationships have sometimes been confrontational because of poorly communicated needs and unmet expectations. Manufacturer-distributor relationships were based on exhaustive contracts which resulted in mutual suspicion. Manufacturers did not believe that distributors sold their products actively. Distributors often believed that manufacturers dumped excessive or unsalable inventory on them. A major benefit of open communication is that the customer's and distributor's expectations can be more aligned, thereby reducing mistrust.

OPEN COMMUNICATION

The major causes of customer-supplier disputes can be attributed to poor communication, poor cooperation, and poor subsequent coordination to resolve root cause disputes. These result in confusion that inevitably begets poor quality, high prices, over promises, under delivery, and inconsistent service.

Variation in any form, including misunderstanding of inconsistent messages, is a major contributor to poor quality. Open communication tends to decrease variation in quality, price, delivery, and performance. Having multiple suppliers exacerbates variation. A major rationale for single source partnering is to ensure the final customer requirements are understood and communicated properly to internal and external suppliers.

Partnering should therefore be based on mutual trust and respect that is established through open communication. This may require a change in organizational mindset. Change is difficult for suppliers who have been providing products and services for many years, because habits become ingrained and change is resisted. Open communication should alleviate many of the major problems concerning poor quality, which may include:

- Poor understanding of what the final customer wants, needs, and expects.
  A company does not understand final customer requirements and these are not communicated to the internal organization.
- Poor internal understanding of technical requirements.
  Once developed, purchasing personnel cannot consistently interpret engineering drawings, specifications, or standards.
- Poor cooperation and communication among internal departments.

Internal groups, such as marketing, engineering, purchasing, manufacturing, and others communicate with each other poorly. Poor internal communication results in inadequately written specifications and purchase orders.

• Poor communication between purchaser and supplier.
Engineering, marketing, or manufacturing may communicate directly with suppliers, bypassing purchasing. When more than one voice communicates, the supplier becomes confused because of mixed signals.

• Poor follow through or no follow through.
Standards and specifications have been established but there is no effort to follow up. If problems arise, there is no coordinated effort to correct and eliminate the root causes of problems.[5]

ELECTRONIC DATA INTERCHANGE (EDI)

Electronic communication of data, usually through Electronic Data Interchange (EDI) is generally thought to be the way for improving communication and information flows among suppliers, carriers, distributors, and internal departments. EDI is the electronic interchange of structured business and technical data among partners. In this way, duplication and mistakes can be eliminated.

The problem is that the publicity and ensuing expectations of EDI surpassed its realized successes. EDI is not easy. EDI fundamentally changes the ways organizations conduct business. Communication is instantaneous and paperless. Business partners and suppliers are reluctant to implement EDI because of its costs, technology complexity, and the organizational changes required to make it work. Also, EDI requires a major investment in time and resources. Users do not reap its full economic and productive benefits if it is imposed or if it is pursued halfheartedly.

Seamless and instantaneous communication, however, is generally thought to be a key to improving quality. The focus of EDI has thus broadened. EDI strictly encompasses transmitting standardized business data, such as forms, among trading partners. A broader concept is emerging that integrates batch and interactive communication using Inter-Enterprise Systems (IES). IES incorporates EDI, intercompany electronic mail, videotex/online databases, facsimile, electronic funds transfer, and exchange of computer aided design and manufacturing graphics, specifications, and documents into a seamless information flow.[6]

GENERAL CUSTOMER QUALITY EXPECTATIONS

Another element of improving communications is that purchasing should serve as the voice of its internal customers, such as engineering or manufacturing, to the supplier base. For purchasing, this is also a two-way process. If there are problems or new developments with suppliers, purchasing serves as the organization's eyes and ears, and communicates these changes internally. Progressive suppliers understand this and work with purchasing to satisfy the final as well as the internal customer's expectations.

As discussed in Chapter 4, companies are developing extensive quality standards that communicate specific requirements to suppliers. The standards developed by the auto industry are models for many organizations.

Specific quality requirements are found in quality standards and are similar to those shown in the last chapter. In general, a supplier embarking on the quality journey is expected to:

- Determine customer requirements.
- Plan how to satisfy these requirements.
- Develop product specifications that result in satisfying customer requirements.
- Pursue companywide continuous improvement.
- Improve at the same rate as the customer.
- Improve end-product performance and reliability.
- Encourage its contractors and suppliers to pursue companywide continuous improvement.
- Prevent problems from occurring.

- Meet specifications without waivers or deviations.
- Inform the customer of problems.
- Meet delivery targets.
- Reduce end-product costs.
- Share gains with the customer.
- Work with the customer to build long-term trust.
- Train all personnel in quality.
- Establish benchmarks and measure all critical processes.

FAIRNESS, RESPECT, AND GOODWILL

Quality improvement and partnering requires a mindset that is based on mutual fairness, respect, and good will. If an adversarial relationship is maintained, then at the first sign of a problem, one party won't go the extra step, or may seek a temporary advantage over the other party. As a result, the relationship sours.

Quality improvement through partnering is intrinsically a positive goal that both customer and supplier jointly pursue in acknowledgement that either party has more to gain than through an adversarial relationship. On the other hand, a price, cost, or productivity focus tends to create the opposite relationship—hardened, adversarial, and win-lose posturing. While front-end price is important, it is mutually profitable to focus on continuous improvement and overall cost reduction. This long-term strategic perspective aims to ensure customer satisfaction and inevitably, profitability.

In a long-term partnership, the buyer and supplier develop a symbiotic and synergistic relationship. Both parties understand the wants, needs, and requirements of each other. Each party should also understand the risks and responsibilities that go along with the relationship.

BUILDING COMMITMENT

Partnering sounds like a simple relationship of two or more parties getting together for mutual benefit. One would assume that both parties voluntarily enter into a win-win arrangement.

In this mutually secure environment, customer and supplier learn about each others' concerns, wants, and capabilities. Negotiation is more open where price, quality, and delivery are discussed freely. Trust is engendered. Through open communication, market opportunities are revealed and competitive pressures for both parties are lessened.

Partnering, is however, a complex relationship with many reciprocal responsibilities and shared risks/rewards. The reward for both parties is obviously long-term profitability. The risks of poor designs or poor service can lead to customer dissatisfaction, loss of sales, or perhaps even damage awards.

To minimize risks and to build long-term trust, suppliers are asked to follow the continuous improvement process variously called certification, qualification, or partnering. The supplier knows that if quality is not improved, if costs are not reduced, if material is not delivered on time, the supplier eventually will be dropped. Xerox, for example, reduced its supplier base from 5,000 to less than 500 and worked with these suppliers on just-in-time delivery and quality management.[7]

Companywide continuous improvement is more effective if a supplier recognizes its value and adopts the philosophy on its own. If continuous improvement is imposed on suppliers, resentment and ultimately failure will result. Continuous improvement will successfully evolve if it is voluntarily integrated into the supplier's organizational culture. Ultimately, the question "What's in it for me?" must be addressed and answered.

At first, suppliers will develop a trial and very limited improvement effort if it is a condition of retaining the customer's business. They will invest in long-term, continuous improvement only if attainable, tangible benefits can be identified.

Preferably, suppliers can be sold on the internal benefits, such as:

- Improved supplier product quality and reliability.
- Improved manufacturing.
- Improved ability to comply with regulatory standards.
- Reduced field service costs.
- Reduced liability exposure.
- Reduced inventories.

INDUCEMENTS

The supplier certification process is long, costly, and draining. Not all candidate suppliers become a partner. Also, frustrations and tensions arise. Candidate or supplier-partners want to know what's in it for them at each step of the continuous improvement process. The partnership should offer tangible benefits to suppliers. Otherwise, no supplier will want to go through the travail.

Suppliers should understand that along with participation in the trial partnership go certain rewards that are spelled out by the customer. If a supplier is awarded preferred status, the supplier gains exclusive long-term contracts and also gains preferential treatment in new part development and a select position in source selection.

There are a number of additional effective and commonly used inducements to encourage participation in the certification and partnership process. Some of these are as follows:

- High volumes.
  Tying volumes to performance is very effective. The signals to the supplier are immediate and reinforcing. Good supplier performance leads to additional business.
- Long-term contract.
  If a supplier has steadily improved, then a long-term contract reinforces the message of continuous improvement.
- Exclusive contract.
  If supplier performance has been exceptional, then an exclusive contract may be awarded. There are risks, however, that the supplier may not be motivated to improve in the future.
- Award.
  Awards, such as Ford's Q1 designation, or an ad in *The Wall Street Journal*, provide visibility leading to additional business.
- Technical assistance.
  If a component is complex and if the supplier is producing parts to the customer's print, then the customer may supply technical assistance.

- Financial assistance.
  As more companies out-source, they want the supplier to be a extension of their organization. They may provide financial assistance to the supplier to produce a special product.
- Certification.
  A certified partner has its products immediately sent to the production line. This assumes they have few or no defects. Being a certified supplier to a large company leads to additional work.[8]

CONDITIONS OF PARTNERING

The demands on the customer to maintain and improve overall competitiveness are high, and these requirements are passed onto the supplier base. If competitiveness through continued final customer satisfaction is not pursued, then the downside risk to a product manufacturer or service provider is loss of business. To maximize the upside, the supplier-partner understands and agrees to some or all of the following conditions:

- Tighter and higher requirements must be met.
  Continuous improvement is a necessary condition of business in a competitive global economy.
- Partner will be continuously audited.
  The partner is continuously monitored throughout the certification and partnering process.
- Order levels are tied to overall performance.
  Order levels are tied to performance, not only in quality but also in cost, technology, service, and delivery.
- Partner must be flexible.
  Market conditions may change and the partner must be able to adjust to higher or lower demands.
- Operational controls may be imposed.
  As a partner becomes more integrated into the customer's operations, the supplier becomes a natural extension of the customer. The customer may impose internal controls onto the supplier to ensure that the customer's requirements are being met.

TRUE TEST OF PARTNERING

The true test comes when one party needs and requests the special assistance of the other party. The assistance may be midnight delivery of a needed part, after the sale field support in Shanghai, immediate payment of an invoice, or any special favor above and beyond the normal call of business duty.

Commitment to deliver at this point is the true measure of a partnership and, it is hoped, the result of building long-term trust. The natural tendency to seek a comparative advantage when the other party is down must be subordinated to the long-term recognition of mutual gains.

It's good to evaluate the relationship periodically. When organizations ask subordinates to evaluate their supervisors, managers often walk away from this experience both surprised and chastened. Similarly, in the partnership arrangement, it is helpful to ask suppliers to evaluate the customer end of the relationship. Areas of concern can serve as areas for improving the relationship.

NO SURPRISES

Even with the above inducements, a supplier-partner does not want unexpected changes, including change in order levels (both down and up), change in designs, additional features in the product, change in delivery dates, changing lead times, late payments, or cancelled orders. Unexpected or abnormal circumstances cause variation in normal business procedures which create disruptions and result in poor quality. For example, an anticipated design change can mean new tooling. New orders may mean additional overtime, which may breed employee discontent. A canceled order results in a loss of trust. A change in delivery date may mean reshuffling the master schedule and other hassles.

Once inducements are offered, the customer must deliver on promises. This builds trust, which is a prerequisite to long-term quality improvement.

If a supplier provides competitively priced, defect-free products that are delivered just-in-time in a courteous manner and the customer delivers on promises, benefits will accrue to both parties which will translate into mutual sustained profitability.

NOTES

[1]Howard Gitlow and Donald Wiser, "Vendor Relations: An Important Piece of the Quality Puzzle," *Quality Progress*, January 1988, pp. 19–23.

[2]Frank Zaffing, "Contract Manufacturing Can Help." *Manufacturing Systems*, April 1987, pp. 58–60.

[3]Alice Agoos, "Air Products Will Take Care of Motorola's Gas," *Chemical Week*, May 11, 1988, pp. 9–13.

[4]"Partnering is a Strategy—Not a Gizmo for Selling MRO," *Purchasing*, April 28, 1988, pp. 60–71.

[5]See Ross Johnson's and Richard Weber's *Buying Quality*, NY: Franklin Watts, 1985, for an interesting discussion of the importance of quality in purchasing.

[6]Wheatman, V. S., "A Wide-Angle View of the EDI Market," *Business Communications Review*, October 1990, pp 77–81.

[7]Sylvia Tiersten, "The Changing Face of Purchasing," *Electronic Business*, March 20, 1989, pp. 22–27.

[8]For excellent discussions on supplier inducements, refer to *Purchasing Magazine*, from which some of these items were derived.

Chapter Six

Organizing for Partnering

P artnering requires new perspectives and new methods of doing business. For example, when Ford Motor Company successfully used the partnering concept in its Taurus and Sable lines of autos, it emphasized top management commitment, promoted middle management trust and respect, established open lines of communication, encouraged supplier involvement and improvement, and focused on satisfying the final customer.[1] GM's approach was also similar in successful quality efforts for its Buick and Cadillac divisions.

An organization should have its house in order before it can expect suppliers to launch a companywide, continuous improvement effort. The customer's organizational structure may have to be overhauled if its management style is authoritarian, internal groups compete for scarce resources, or internal coordination is poor. In general, the clerical mind-set of purchasing must be destroyed.

To spearhead this effort, purchasing is being elevated to a vice presidential level, to a chief purchasing officer (CPO). The CPO is responsible for communicating partnering commitment and reinforcing these messages to chief executives in the supplier base. If this is not done properly, suppliers will perceive the partnership effort as another special project or exhortation that gets low priority, which is always a prescription for failure.

Internally, the CPO works to reduce departmental barriers that inhibit communication, coordination, and continuous improvement. Especially in technology-intensive industries, communication and cooperation among multidisciplinary teams that incorporate key suppliers are essential to new product development. No one person, department, or supplier has the requisite knowledge, experience, or skills to quickly develop state of the art products. Teams must work together to optimize quality, cost, delivery, and service objectives so that there is always a satisfied final customer. To do this, everyone's focus is on the common vision of customer satisfaction, not on aggrandizing individual accomplishments or winning turf battles.

In a similar move, Texas Instruments Incorporated initiated the key executive concept, where key suppliers are asked to dedicate a key manager to be the point person for directing the partnership. These executives demonstrate their commitment to partnering by eliminating organizational obstacles to continuous improvement and by enhancing communication between the parties.[2]

While purchasing is being centralized at a high level to coordinate company and supplier wide matters, many other purchasing responsibilities are being decentralized. At the corporate level, purchasing directs supplier matters, such as integrating suppliers into product development teams, negotiating systems contracts, and buying specialized or commodity goods. At a business unit or plant level, buyers and agents are responsible for day-to-day operations. Front line buyers are thus in the best position to purchase specific components, raw material, and capital equipment used in a plant's production because they are closer to what users, the internal customers, want and need. Also, they have firsthand information on supplier quality, price, delivery, and technology.

PROJECT AND CONTRACT MANAGEMENT

In partnering, buyers evolve into project managers and contract administrators responsible for monitoring a partner's performance and improvement. Instead of buying components based solely on price, a buyer will work with world class partners with specialized knowledge to design parts or assemblies for the next generation of products.

Many organizations are funneling technical specialists and operations people into purchasing. Specialists have expertise in law, accounting, or design. Operations people know how products are produced. The problem of not being technically oriented is especially exacerbated in electronic buying by fast changing technology, the critical nature of product reliability, and long lead times.

Another development is the emerging role of entrepreneurial purchasing. To instill the urgency of internal customer service, buyers, agents, and managers charge internal clients an hourly rate for their services. The rate structure reflects overheads, salaries, administrative expenses, and a sufficient profit margin. Any profit at the end of the year is distributed to purchasing's employees as an incentive bonus.

Do these types of programs work? Sometimes, it is difficult to take employees and supervisors who were hired, trained, nurtured, rewarded, and promoted to be risk averse, and then expect them to be entrepreneurial, internal customer driven, and risk taking.

COMMIT TO CHANGE

Establishing a supplier partnership is difficult. Purchasing personnel become tired, discouraged, and frustrated. Everyone's responsibility increases and hours are long. If management is not sensitive to this, burn out can set in.

Internal change can't simply be mandated from above. Quality awareness and commitment to continuous improvement must be fostered and internalized before being communicated to suppliers. If the buyer or agent talking to suppliers daily does not believe the messages of continuous improvement, it won't be heard by the supplier. This can become a major hindrance.

Change is difficult and disruptive. The process should be gradual. An awareness of the urgency for change must first be created. Awareness is created by destroying the clerical mind-set of simply taking orders and negotiating lowest price contracts. Purchasing people must understand that this mind-set is the road to professional obsolescence. People should also be provided with the tools to change. Only then can intelligent risk taking be encouraged, nurtured, and rewarded.

CREATING AWARENESS AND BUILDING COMMITMENT

Commitment for change starts from top management because only they can authorize changes in policy and institute training. Top management commitment may sound like a wish list to those stuck in glorified clerical positions. But many leading edge organizations like Eastman Kodak Co. realize that customer satisfaction through continuous improvement is a survival issue. At Kodak, quality is implemented beyond simple customer satisfaction. It involves the total customer experience with the product, including delivery, performance, and service. To insure organizational flexibility and attention to the final customer, each line manager has an annual quality improvement objective that is part of his or her overall performance evaluation.[3]

One way to create an urgency in purchasing is to survey internal customer departments and ask people to evaluate internal communication, coordination, and cooperation. Results always reveal how little the left hand of the organization talks to the right hand. Internal groups become aware that they are truly internal customers of each other.

Internal commitment to continuous improvement is created by education and training, not by indoctrination or exhortation. Studies indicate quality has to be incorporated into the customer's and partner's culture. The authoritarian management style discussed in the previous chapter makes it difficult to communicate and reinforce the messages of continuous improvement and partnering.

An AT&T study concluded that the quality concept relates strongly to personal feelings of succeeding, failing, and meeting expectations of others. The study found that quality messages such as "do it right the first time" and "zero defects" can be viewed negatively.[4]

Organizational development principles properly deployed can be used to build the necessary commitment. These principles include:

- Fully using everyone's skills, abilities and talents.
- Encouraging learning and growing.
- Encouraging and rewarding risk taking.
- Encouraging individual responsibility in terms of providing a socially valuable product or service.
- Encouraging having fun.[5]

An organization can also increase purchasing effectiveness by upgrading jobs, rewarding exceptional involvement, developing quality-based compensation systems, and training personnel. Corporate commitment can also be reinforced by eliminating unnecessary regulations and barriers to initiative.

ADDITIONAL KNOWLEDGE

Not too many years ago, purchasing people were considered the business experts who handled contract negotiations on price and delivery of products and services. Purchasing personnel did not need to know what they were buying because they subordinated technical matters to engineering or manufacturing. In many organizations, this is considered the road to professional obsolescence.

To succeed in the partnering environment, purchasing people must be more aware of how a product is designed and made. Therefore, they have to be introduced to a new set of management tools. Traditional tools of purchasing involved knowledge of costing, product lines, negotiating skills, computer skills, and the Uniform Commercial Code (UCC). Now, knowledge in quality management, statistical techniques, Just-In-Time, process manufacturing, and engineering is required. This is difficult and scary for many purchasing people who claim special expertise in their profession and do not want to venture into new areas.

Training requires an investment of time and monies. Motorola invested $40 million in training employees in 1986 alone. Much of the training covered quality improvement, designing for manufacturability, and improving service. Since 30 to 60 percent of the sales dollar of some Motorola product lines is out-sourced, suppliers are also partners in this training.[6]

GETTING STARTED

The continuous improvement effort requires time, resources, planning, and direction. Before embarking on the improvement journey with suppliers, the customer should ask:

- Where are am I going?
- What road will take me there?
- What are the milestones of the journey?
- How am I going to get there?
- Who's in charge?
- What resources are needed to get there?
- How long will it take to reach each milestone?

These questions are fundamental to any business endeavor. They deal with strategy, objectives, plans, accountabilities, resources, costs, timelines, and benchmarks. If the above questions are not asked, the customer's team will eventually flounder. The supplier wanting to partner will receive mixed or incorrect messages, which may reflect in unsatisfactory product or service quality.

It should be mentioned that there is no set of right answers to the above questions. The questions depend on the industry, the customer's organizational culture, product lines, supplier base, technical capabilities, and human resource capabilities. A general roadmap for getting started in the continuous improvement effort may involve the following steps:

- Establish a team.
- Develop an action plan.
- Develop specifications and standards.
- Prioritize product attributes.
- Determine process control and capability.
- Measure performance.
- Improve continuously.
- Take ownership.
- Audit performance.

ESTABLISH A TEAM

Many internal voices want to communicate with suppliers. Unfortunately, many voices create confusion and deliver mixed messages. The way to dispel confusion is to create a multidisciplinary team of internal users who can distill requirements so that the organization can speak with one voice to the supplier base. It is essential that all key internal customers meet as early as possible to identify and spell out the requirements of the final customer, as well as internal requirements.

DEVELOP AN ACTION PLAN

A customer should start with one supplier or a select group of suppliers in a pilot effort. A pilot is recommended because the continuous improvement ethic may be new to the customer's and supplier's organizations. Mistakes will be made. Misunderstandings will occur. If problems are small, isolated, and manageable, they can be resolved amicably and effectively. They will not infect other supplier relationships. Over time, the lessons and tactics learned in the pilot can then be applied to all suppliers.

DEVELOP SPECIFICATIONS AND STANDARDS

Continuous improvement can be achieved only if the customer sets and communicates explicit standards and measures for quality, delivery, service, and cost. The supplier should be able to understand, and not have to interpret, quality standards and specifications. Standards should be current, accurate, complete, measurable, and realistic.

A major source of defects and poor communication is poor engineering drawings. Consistent quality conformance and performance can result only if the drawings include all the required information about the application of the product, the environment in which it is used, realistic tolerances, performance requirements, and components with which they will interact. If not, problems will arise because these documents spell out customer requirements to suppliers.

Once these have been established, the customer and supplier should ensure that both parties speak the same measurement language. This includes identifying the appropriate unit of measurement, obtaining comparably accurate and precise equipment, and training inspectors to measure and test similarly.

PRIORITIZE PRODUCT ATTRIBUTES

A product can have many quality attributes. Important product quality characteristics should be identified on the engineering print. The supplier is expected to provide SPC charts and to control the processes that made these designated quality characteristics. Only those product dimensions or attributes that are important or have impact on product performance should initally be process controlled. Thus, prioritizing quality characteristics focuses the supplier's attention on what the customer deems important.

Some companies prioritize quality characteristics in terms of critical, major, and minor quality attributes. Nonconforming critical characteristics can jeopardize health, safety, or welfare. Nonconforming major characteristics affect product function. A minor product nonconformance, a blemish, deals with product appearance.

DETERMINE PROCESS CONTROL AND CAPABILITY

Once a commonly understood measurement system has been devised and product characteristics have been prioritized, the supplier is asked to submit a process flow diagram and specify the most suitable locations for tracking quality and testing products. The supplier establishes effective statistical process controls to the designated product quality characteristics. Sometimes, the supplier is asked to use SPC at the process locations that produced the product dimensions measured in incoming material inspection.

A supplier first develops limited process controls and, over time, expands the controls to include noncritical operations as the supplier becomes more integrated with the customer. SPC has a cumulative effect on improving product quality. A product may be the result of a process of 100 steps. By first focusing on the critical, and then major product characteristics, eventually all of a product's important characteristics will be produced by controlled and capable processes.

If the supplier does not have statistical systems in place, the process may be slow. Managers, supervisors, and operators must be trained and data capturing equipment may be purchased. A supplier may understand the concepts of customer satisfaction and defect prevention, but it takes time to understand and internalize the concept of continuous improvement through minimizing variation.

Once a process is in statistical control, the supplier can determine whether the process is capable of meeting customer's specifications. If there is a nonconformance, the supplier is expected to segregate the nonconforming material, and to report the nonconformance to the customer. The supplier is also expected to have a system that will quickly and accurately correct the symptom and the root cause of the nonconformance.

MEASURE PERFORMANCE

In the continuous improvement process, performance measures are essential. To improve continuously, benchmarks and timelines have to be set and improvements measured. The measurement system indicates how quickly improvement is being pursued.

Common measures of supplier performance are:

- Process capability.
- Life-cycle costs.
- Cost of quality.
- Service levels.
- Delivery targets.
- Defects per product.
- Defectives per shipment.
- Rejected shipments.
- Late or early shipments.
- Production stoppages due to poor quality.
- Final customer complaints.
- Customer satisfaction levels.
- Amount of material accepted on-waivers.
- Scrap and rework.
- Warranty costs due to product failure.

The appropriate measure to use depends on the type of product, customer's expectations, and the level of quality systems the supplier has in place. Defects per product or defectives per shipment are mainly used in incoming material inspection. If a supplier has just started SPC, process capability is preferred. If the supplier has extensive quality systems, life-cycle cost and customer satisfaction indices are important measures.

Federal Express, a recent National Quality Award winner, tracks and measures 12 service factors which it has identified as being critical to customer satisfaction. As with most continuous improvement efforts, a multifunctional team works to reduce the number of failures in each of the following 12 service categories:

- Wrong date late.
- Right day late.
- Invoice adjustment requested.
- Telephone traces.
- Damaged packages.
- Missing proofs of delivery on invoices.
- Complaints reopened.

- Overgoods.
- Abandoned calls.
- Lost packages.
- Missed pickups.
- International business.[7]

Front-end price, a commonly used measure, is a disarming number if a flawed product causes injuries or if discourteous service causes customer dissatisfaction. The total cost of using, maintaining and repairing a defective product or having to settle a service problem can totally distort front-end price.

IMPROVE CONTINUOUSLY

In a narrow sense, continuous improvement means that performance or specification targets have been set and over time, variation around these targets is gradually reduced. The bell shaped curve is centered at the specification target and the curve becomes narrower with a higher peak.

In a broader sense, the supplier is asked to define achievable and measurable companywide targets of performance and to reduce variation around these targets. At some point, the supplier may be asked to establish and maintain a system for controlling the quality of its supplied materials. Its suppliers (supplier's suppliers) may be asked to initiate a pilot effort controlling physical, chemical, visual, and functional requirements and then to expand the effort into other organizational areas.

Once the pilot has proven successful, the continuous improvement effort is expanded to incorporate all first tier suppliers. The long-term intent is to integrate all product and service suppliers into the continuous improvement chain.

TAKE OWNERSHIP

Once the customer has initiated the improvement effort, the supplier is encouraged and induced to take ownership of the improvement effort and be responsible for it. Ford Motor Co. suppliers are expected to proactively pursue continuous improvement through a quality planning process involving the following:

- Organize a cross functional team for managing the quality planning process.
- Establish a timing chart to monitor progress.
- Determine customer needs and expectations.
- Verify that design requirements are feasible for the selected manufacturing process at specified volumes.
- Develop a manufacturing system and control plans to assure product requirements are met and maintained with statistical evidence of process control.
- Verify the adequacy of the manufacturing system and control plans from an evaluation of a production trial run.
- Sign off on a quality planning process that successfully demonstrates the ability to produce ongoing quality.[8]

AUDIT PERFORMANCE

An inevitable result of the continuous improvement effort is that only a few suppliers will have the commitment and stamina for the long haul. Often the biggest challenge for a supplier is the ability to adapt and adopt a new style of doing business. Remaining suppliers evolve into supplier-partners and in some cases single source partners. With one or a few suppliers, the customer can more easily explain its requirements and take the time to build a long-term relationship.

There are risks, however, when a customer selects a single source partner. The partner may not improve in areas important to the customer or improve quickly enough. To ensure the partner and customer are closely aligned, the partner is periodically audited. The audits assure the customer that the supplier's internal systems and actions satisfy its requirements.

It is sometimes said that auditing is counterproductive to the premise of building trust. Even in a long-term partnering relationship, the supplier is periodically audited to verify continuous improvement. The next chapter discusses important factors to consider in chosing a supplier-partner.

NOTES

[1]John Simmons, "Partnering Pulls Everything Together," *Journal for Quality & Participation*, June 1989, pp. 12–16.

[2]Cathy Handley, "Teamwork of a Global Nature," *Purchasing*, October 27, 1988, pp. 76–77.

[3]Colby Chandler, "Quality: Beyond Customer Satisfaction," *Quality Progress*, February 1989, pp. 30–32.

[4]James Lader, "Getting Emotional About Quality," *Quality Progress*, July 1988, pp. 16–18.

[5]Alexander Philip, "Quality's Third Dimension," *Quality Progress*, July 1988, pp. 21–23.

[6]Shirley Cayer, "World Class Suppliers Don't Grow on Trees," *Purchasing*, August 25, 1988, p. 46.

[7]Derived from Federal Express seminar material.

[8]"Planning for Quality," Ford Motor Co., 1990.

Chapter Seven

Partner Selection

T his chapter and the next discuss two important elements of the partnering process. This chapter examines supplier-partner selection and evaluation. The next chapter discusses partnership building.

Supplier partnering has forced a radical shift in purchasing philosophy. In the near future, the customer will carefully select supplier-partners, integrate them into product development, monitor their rate of improvement and overall performance, and promote a long-term, mutually profitable relationship. Product availability and low price will no longer solely dictate supplier choice. Management attitudes, manufacturing process controls, and engineering capabilities will be equally important when establishing a long-term partnering relationship.

The method of selecting and evaluating most suppliers follows a similar pattern. The details are obviously different depending on the type of product, application, user environment, level of technology, and product value.

RATING SUPPLIERS

During the selection, certification, and partnering process, suppliers are periodically evaluated on criteria that usually involve quality, cost, technology, and service. Up to five years ago, price, not quality was the most important factor in selecting and evaluating suppliers. Now, quality consists of 40 to 70 percent of the buy decision. The changes in selection criteria can be seen in Table 7–1.

Selection criteria and their ratings, incorporated into a quality standard, can vary. Some quality standards have just three criteria: quality, price, and service. At Texas Instruments, the criteria and their ratings are: quality, 40 percent; delivery, 25 percent; pricing, 20 percent; and service, 15 percent.

Many companies are adopting the Malcolm Baldrige National Quality Award criteria, which is broken down into seven quality related elements as shown in Table 7–2.

TABLE 7–1
Changes in Selection Criteria

Selection Criteria	Ratings Five Years Ago	Selection Criteria	Ratings Now
Cost	50–70%	Quality	40–70%
Service	20–30	Cost	30–40
Availability	10–20	Service/Delivery	10–20
Quality	10–20	Technology	10–20

TABLE 7–2
Malcolm Baldrige National Quality Award Criteria

Category	Percentage
1. Leadership	10
2. Information and analysis	7
3. Strategic quality planning	6
4. Human resource utilization	15
5. Quality assurance of products and service	14
6. Quality results	18
7. Customer satisfaction	30
Total	100

The ranking of the criteria may change, depending on customer requirements and the type of product. For example, in the mature copier industry, customers are more concerned with service than quality, technology, or price, so service would receive a higher rating than price. Copier suppliers are expected to provide extensive service agreements because downtime is exasperating to customers. Most copiers are already reliable and have high-tech features. Even low-end copiers have high-tech features such as reduction, enlargement, and collating abilities. More expensive, high-end copiers can interface with other machines, which allows users to scan, digitize, reformulate, receive, store, retransit, enhance, and edit images.[1]

QUALITY STANDARDS

As discussed, poor communication results in poor coordination and cooperation, which inevitably begets poor quality and dissatisfied final customers. Internal customers, who specify or use supplied products and services, must assess their requirements and then develop crystal clear statements of need.

Once distilled into a quality standard or similar document, purchasing communicates these statements to existing and prospective suppliers. A customer wish list is dangerous and should be avoided at all costs. It indicates sloppy thinking that seems to result in customer dissatisfaction because some perceived need is not fulfilled.

QUALITY STANDARDS

In Chapter 4, the evolution of continuous improvement was illustrated through several quality standards. The standards are very common. Most large organizations use them to evaluate and monitor suppliers. They can be generated in several ways. An organization can adopt an existing standard, such as the standard of one's most stringent customer or strongest competitor. From the supplier's point of view, if the organization can comply with this standard, then it probably can comply with its other customers' quality requirements.

Or an organization can gather all of its internal users to develop a generic standard for all products, or develop a standard tailored to each product line. Another option is to use generic boilerplate from existing standards, then develop sections addressing specific process or product characteristics. Either way, internal customers have an opportunity to express their needs and concerns.

Sometimes, products and systems are so complex that consultants with specialized expertise, regulatory or industry knowledge are retained to draw up technical specifications and quality standards. Examples of these complex products are PBX phone systems, military hardware, turnkey projects, computer-integrated manufacturing (CIM) systems, and software.

Software and Hardware Specifications
The need for specialized input, either from consultants or internal users, can be illustrated by the process of purchasing computer hardware and software. In evaluating hardware, important technical and quality factors to consider include processing speed, size of random access memory, size of permanent memory, connectivity with other hardware, access time, portability, and customer support.

Computer hardware compared with software has almost become an inexpensive commodity. As a general rule, every two years hardware costs are reduced by half as software costs increase.

Customers want software to solve specific problems. From the customer's point of view, three factors stand out in distinguishing user friendly from bad software: (1) ease of use, (2) documentation, and (3) service/support. In determining "good" software, the following special quality criteria would be incorporated in engineering specifications and a specialized quality standard:

- Software compatibility with the hardware.
- Software compatibility with other operating software.

- Understandable supporting documentation.
- Training by the supplier or by third parties.
- User friendly software that loads easily.
- Menu-driven.
- Understandable on-screen diagnostics.
- Informative graphics output.
- Ability of the user to extend the useful life of software through updating software parameters or through service updates offered by the supplier.
- Provisions for data security and integrity.[2]

The last item in the above list, "provisions for data security and integrity," refers to computer reliability. Many commercial businesses use interconnecting, networking, and electronic transferring technologies to conduct business. As recent news stories attest, a software virus has been able to disrupt a major computer system or cause a major system malfunction. A computer security violation in a financial institution recently destroyed financial records and in another case provided unauthorized people access to confidential information.[3]

SUPPLIER EVALUATION

A buyer usually cannot go to an industrial register and find a key product partner who will share in risks and rewards throughout the development and product life cycles. The process is more convoluted, requiring extensive upfront research and evaluation.

For a new contract, the first challenge is to develop a list of prospective domestic or offshore suppliers. A buyer can develop a list of domestic sources by talking to industry contacts, referring to business registers, searching manufacturer's catalogs, thumbing through phone books, visiting trade shows, and browsing through trade journal advertisements. An offshore list of suppliers can be generated by contacting trade representatives, the U.S. Chamber of Commerce, foreign consulates, the U.S. Commerce Department, and the U.S. State Department.

The next step is to narrow the supplier list. Prospective suppliers are sent a survey audit form and asked to evaluate their own quality, service, and technology. This is often a cursory yes/no survey form. The team, composed of internal customers, assesses the supplier's self-evaluation. Based on evaluation results, the team may authorize an on-site visit to verify the information provided on the survey form and to clarify issues and questions raised during the evaluation.

In the on-site visit, an auditor or audit team reviews the supplier's facilities and operating units, interviews corporate officials, and reviews internal quality system controls. This is especially important in dealing with foreign suppliers because the assessment may reveal future problems dealing with such factors as language, culture, delivery, and laws.

Early involvement brings all user groups together to consider the relative importance of the material or services being bought. Bringing all the users together to reach a consensus decision makes good political sense. This reduces the possibility that someone may later carp that he or she was not consulted in the choice of suppliers.

Supplier performance can be evaluated at regular intervals or when an unusual situation arises. Supplier monitoring is discussed in the next chapter. Usually, if a supplier provides an entire product line, each component or assembly is evaluated or qualified separately.

A list of quality related factors often considered when evaluating suppliers includes:

- Senior management attitudes.
  If a supplier's senior management is concerned with the issues of partnering, customer satisfaction, and continuous improvement, this attitude will be communicated and will prevail throughout the supplier's organization.
- Progressive management.
  The goals of customer satisfaction and continuous improvement require progressive supplier management. Conservative, risk averse management bodes poorly for an effort that requires flexibility and a change in operating focus.

- Motivation to improve continuously.
  Motivation and an attitude of cooperation by all the supplier's employees reflect positively on the desire to improve.
- Focus on the final customer.
  To many companies, customer satisfaction is the latest buzzword and ad puffery. A company must go beyond words and show commitment by action. Daily problems are always solvable if the goal is to satisfy the final customer and issues are subordinated to this goal.
- Companywide quality management.
  Customer satisfaction and continuous improvement can only be achieved if the entire organization cooperates and communicates.
- Ability to add value.
  A supplier's ability to add value to a transaction, product, or service is also essential.
- Supplier performance history.
  Past performance is a good indicator of future performance. Of course, when a continuous improvement effort is being initiated, there is no supplier history to evaluate. Past motivation, however, as well as attitudes and cooperation all provide a clue as to how a continuous improvement effort will be pursued.
- Just-in-time delivery.
  JIT delivery is a service related factor. JIT is often the next step after defect-free quality has been achieved by suppliers. In the past, JIT was pursued before high-quality levels were achieved by suppliers, which resulted in problems.
- Supplier location.
  JIT and partnering require that suppliers deliver material within tight time windows. For certain products, suppliers located nearby or near transportation hubs can communicate easier and deliver material more consistently than offshore suppliers.
- Financial stability.
  Financial stability means a supplier has been a going concern over a period of time. This provides a level of

assurance that the supplier will not suffer liquidity problems, or worse, bankruptcy.

- Technical expertise and equipment.
  Technical ability is required to design and manufacture state of the art products. Engineers design, simulate use and test products on computer-aided design (CAD) systems. These systems generate prints that are distributed to key supplier partners. Instructions are downloaded to production machines. Test equipment automatically checks and controls machines.

- Research and development.
  Product life cycles are short. To feed the new product pipeline, a supplier should have a substantial R&D effort. As suppliers are integrated into product development, suppliers must also be capable of designing and testing state of the art products.

- Production facilities.
  The following questions are important in regard to production facilities. Is the supplier capable of meeting customer specifications? Are critical internal processes under control and is the concept of variation understood by everyone?

- Clean facilities.
  Good housekeeping, a clean work environment, is a reflection of the management that runs the plant or office. Messiness implies sloppy thinking, poor work habits, and disorganization, which may affect future product or service quality.

- Third party registration.
  Registration by an accredited third party organization provides assurance to the customer of a supplier's quality systems. In the 1990s, European companies may require registration in ISO 9000 as a condition of business.

SERVICE PROVIDERS

The objectives of continuous improvement and customer satisfaction are also used to evaluate service providers. The *Wall*

Street Journal recently reported that GM's general counsel wants to reduce the number of outside law firms from 700 to 200 within two years. The firms with the best chance of winning GM's business are those delivering the highest quality service at the lowest cost.[4]

BENCHMARKING

Many supplier selection strategies are based on the premise of identifying and developing world-class suppliers. Is the term *world-class* just another buzzword to sustain competitiveness? No. Many companies are evaluating suppliers in terms of being the best in a class of product suppliers or service deliverers.

A benchmark is usually a world-class performance standard which is used to compare a supplier's products and processes against the best in the world. A benchmark can be a competitor's product, management system, process, quality level, service level, aesthetic design, or cost structure.

Once the factors critical to the success of the world-class competitor's product or process are identified and understood, this information is used to develop internal plans to attain and surpass the best in the world. Benchmarking forces an organization to focus on internal operations that may have been disregarded for years and to ask how these can be improved.

Benchmarking as a philosophy is gaining many new adherents. Benchmarking implies that continuously higher improvement targets can be established and reached. The targets can be in terms of quality, cost, design, or other criteria. Xerox, a recent winner of the National Quality Award, at one time had a reject rate of 10,000 parts per million (PPM) on purchased products. Through benchmarking and continuous improvement, Xerox progressively reduced its defect rate to 5000, 1300, 950, 325, and much lower PPM levels.

QUALITY FUNCTION DEPLOYMENT

Designers use such market research tools as demographic analyses, consumer surveys, focus groups, interviews, warranty cards, and quality function deployment (QFD) to gauge the market and forecast future needs.

A recent mechanism for communicating customer expectations so that they can be incorporated early in the development cycle is quality function deployment (QFD). The premise behind QFD is that the voice of the final customer must be deployed throughout the customer's and key supplier-partner's organizations to ensure that the final customer is satisfied.[5]

DISTRIBUTORS

The distribution side of the supplier equation is often neglected. Many manufacturers market through small distributors. The manufacturers forget that an excellent product reputation can suffer if a distributor's delivery and service are poor.

A small distributor can be a storefront with several trucks and minimal inventory. Distributors may offer lower pricing because offshore products are carried. A small distributor may not understand the importance of quality products, reliable delivery, and prompt technical support. Quality becomes an afterthought.

SUPPLIER PARTNERING PROCESS

Partnering has gained much momentum in recent years. Companies feeling a sense of market desperation are more and more seeking single source, worldclass partners. Several strategies that are being followed in identifying and developing these worldclass partners are discussed in this section. They are:

- Evolutionary.
- Step progression.
- Ramp progression.

The strategies are illustrated in Figure 7–1. Sometimes, a combination of two strategies are used.

EVOLUTIONARY

In the evolutionary approach, the customer and suppliers simultaneously evolve a continuous improvement effort. This is

**FIGURE 7–1
Supplier Partnering Process**

Evolutionary

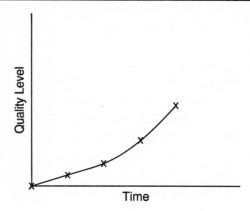

Step Progression

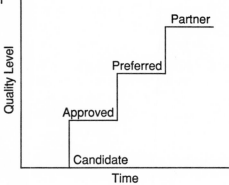

Ramp Progression

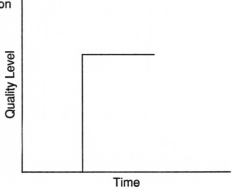

similar to the effort described at the end of the last chapter. If the customer has not evolved any internal quality systems, the customer starts its own continuous improvement effort and then initiates a pilot SPC project with one supplier or a small group of suppliers. A supplier is asked to monitor and statistically control one or more production processes. The supplier provides the customer SPC charts certifying that critical or designated product quality characteristics are monitored and controlled. Over time, more suppliers are asked and induced to adopt statistically driven, companywide prevention techniques and to improve at the same rate as the customer.

Integration into Product Development
If the supplier has been involved in the continuous improvement process for years and is considered worldclass, it should have extensive quality and technical systems that are in place and operating successfully. This supplier can often be incorporated into the customer's product development team without going through the extensive evaluation described in the previous section. Whether the customer is dealing with an existing or new supplier, the customer can feel secure that the supplier has proven capabilities to provide the quality, technology, and service required in the new contract. The customer's advantage in bringing a supplier into the product development process is that the supplier will know exactly what the customer wants and can anticipate the resources needed to satisfy the customer.

Recently at its Saturn plant, GM selected some of its suppliers four years before production started. Selected suppliers had time to review customer requirements to determine manufacturability and to anticipate and solve possible problems. Many suppliers were asked to design an entire assembly in which they had special expertise. With early integration, these suppliers had time to prevent defects and provide valuable design input to GM.[6]

STEP PROGRESSION

Another method is called supplier certification or qualification. This process, illustrated in Figure 7–1b, can be characterized as a series of successively higher steps that a supplier must climb. The certification process can be used to evaluate prospective suppliers for new contracts and to evaluate existing suppliers as they progress to full partnership status. At the highest level, a supplier partner has an extensive continuous improvement program and has become either a single source supplier or one of several supplier-partners for a product line.

Suppliers are awarded a score based on the results of an audit. The score determines if the supplier is a candidate, approved, or preferred supplier. If the specified level of performance has not been attained by a specified date, the supplier is often dropped. Each level indicates where the supplier's products will go, whether into inspection or directly onto the assembly line. At the highest level of certification, a supplier is considered a partner.

At the beginning of the partnering courtship, a customer may train suppliers in SPC, design of experiments, just-in-time delivery, design for manufacturability, and other areas. As the partnering effort evolves, suppliers become responsible for developing new training courses. The purpose of this initial training is to level out the supplier field so that all suppliers have an even chance to be certified partners. Competition is very intense. It is amazing, but at this stage, the customer can usually detect which suppliers are motivated to be certified as a "ship to assembly" partner.

You may say that the partnership idea is good. What happens however if the customer does not have the leverage to encourage or request a partnership? Partnerships should not be imposed unilaterally upon suppliers. Motivation for a partnering arrangement should be a recognition of the mutual wins involved in the relationship.

Uniform and Progressively Higher Standards

There is no commonly agreed upon criteria for certifying suppliers. However, the American Society for Quality Control's (ASQC) Customer Supplier Technical Committee has identified nine minimum certification criteria. Specifically, these are as follows:

1. No product-related rejections over a period of time, usually 12 months.
2. No nonproduct-related rejections for a period of time.
3. No production-related negative incidents for a period of time, usually six months.
4. Successful passing of an on-site quality system evaluation.
5. An agreed upon specification.
6. Documented process and quality system.
7. Ability to furnish timely copies of certificates of analysis, inspection data, and test results.
8. Correlation and validation of laboratory results so that the customer can use supplier's results as it would its own in certification of bulk suppliers.
9. Demonstration of SPC by piece part or assembly suppliers.[7]

What if a supplier has many products and plants? Usually, a supplier is certified for a specific product or product line. If a plant is producing more than one product, then it is conceivable that the plant is fully certified for one product and no others.

Supplier performance is evaluated and monitored periodically. The certification process is time-consuming, especially if each time a product is altered or modified significantly, the certification process should start over again. If the supplier has the management, quality, technical, and service systems in place, then it is much easier to be certified for a new product or a new process.

TQE Selection Process

Ford Motor Co.'s Total Quality Excellence supplier selection, illustrated in Figure 7–2, offers another glimpse into how the certification process is pursued. Ford's first tier suppliers started as candidates and then progressed to earn Ford's highest level award, the Q1. All first tier suppliers are expected to be certified to this level or else they will soon start losing business. Once suppliers have achieved this level, then the process starts again where they must achieve the Total Quality Excellence (TQE) award.

FIGURE 7–2
TQE

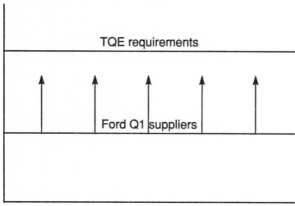

The process for the TQE starts with a self-assessment. If the supplier has achieved a sufficiently high score in the self-assessment, then the supplier petitions Ford for an on site verification audit. Specifically, to achieve the TQE award, Ford suppliers must follow these steps:

- TQE is awarded on a commodity basis.
- Suppliers must have been awarded a Q1 status for at least a year.
- Suppliers must be free of validated quality or initial sample rejections for at least six months.
- Supplier self-evaluation must exceed rating of 90 percent on the quality system, engineering, commercial, and delivery survey criteria.
- If the above have been met, a supplier may petition its Ford Motor Co. buyer for consideration for the award.
- To justify the petition, suppliers must document the self-evaluation and demonstrate that continuous improvement systems are in place.
- A Ford team from quality, engineering, material planning and control, and purchasing assesses the supplier's self-evaluation.

- If the supplier meets all requirements, then a Ford multidisciplinary team visits the supplier for an on-site verification.
- If verified, supplier's qualifications are presented to the Ford Management TQE Committee for approval.
- Every two years, any TQE award recipient must reapply to confirm continuous improvement.[8]

It's interesting to note that all Q1 suppliers who already have excellent quality and have been pursuing continuous improvement for years, must now compete for the higher award. Also, a TQE supplier cannot rest on its laurels because, as the last point indicates, every two years any TQE recipient must reapply to confirm continuous improvement.

RAMP UP

The ramp up strategy, illustrated in Figure 7–1, can be compared to a process of survival of the fittest. In this process, the supplier is expected to achieve a high level of quality performance very quickly. Those who do continue to obtain business; those who do not are dropped as suppliers. If the supplier has pursued a continuous improvement effort for some time, it is obviously easier for the supplier to achieve higher standards of quality.

Many companies are coveting the Malcolm Baldrige National Quality Award. The award criteria listed in Chapter 4 specifies that product and service suppliers should also be adopting quality management techniques. So, many companies are asking suppliers to apply for the award and be examined by the National Quality Award auditors.

Unfortunately, suppliers sometimes take a cynical attitude and apply for the award to placate the customer. The supplier invests money, time, and effort in the superficial elements of the National Quality Award criteria. The purpose of the National Quality Award, however, is to highlight areas of improvement. The quick fix does not work. It takes years for a companywide quality ethic to evolve.

THE PREFERRED METHOD

Is there a preferred method for integrating suppliers into a quality improvement effort? The evolutionary progression is often preferred. Change is gradual and nonthreatening. Internal groups have time to distill requirements. Suppliers have the time to develop a closer relationship with the customer.

The escalation of customer requirements is often dictated by the competitiveness of the marketplace. If the customer faces stiff competition from foreign or domestic firms in terms of high quality, lower price, faster delivery, aesthetic design, or courteous service, then the messages to suppliers are communicated more rigorously and involve a ramp or step progression. The customer will spell out requirements, performance benchmarks to be achieved within a specific timeline. Those that achieve these benchmarks are retained. Those that fail are removed from the bidder's list.

Supplier continuous improvement eventually evolves so that partners become an extension of the customer in certain critical operations. To what extent should this process occur? In some critical operations, suppliers become captive, supplying products to one customer. A notable example is the many Japanese assembly plants that have brought their key supplier-partners to the United States and have moved them next to their operations.

CERTIFYING NEW SUPPLIERS

Many partnering or certification programs have been in place for five or more years. How does a new supplier qualify? The quick answer is: with difficulty. It is very difficult to displace an existing supplier that has extensive quality systems in place and that has provided the customer with competitively priced, quality products and service. Any new supplier must have similar or higher quality, service, and delivery systems as the single supplier-partner.

Can a new supplier obtain part of the business of a supplier-partner? If the single supplier-partner has been improving continuously and has satisfied all of the mutually negotiated goals, then it is difficult for a new supplier to gain any of the business. If sourcing is limited to two suppliers and if one of the suppliers is not meeting the customer's goals, then this supplier may be dropped and the other supplier receives the additional business. Or, the contract may be rebid.

COST COMPETITIVE QUALITY

Ford Motor Co.'s stated goal in its Total Quality Excellence award is: "Ford Motor Company's vision is to be a low-cost producer of the highest quality products and services which provide the best customer value." As the quality of goods and services becomes uniformly high, the total cost of buying, maintaining, servicing, and retiring the product will assume more importance in the selection decision.

Buying solely on the basis of front-end price is now generally recognized as one of the worst possible purchasing decisions. This purchasing decision implies that the costs associated with the product throughout its useful life, its life-cycle costs, have been neglected or are not being considered. Front-end price is a short-term focus that may well result in a much higher total cost and risk than the initial product price.

This can be illustrated by the following example. A supplier may low ball a bid to get business. The bid is for a stripped down, no features version of a product. The product only performs limited functions in a restricted environment. If the buyer wants to expand the product's use, buy additional products, purchase add ons, extend customer support, repair a defective product after the warranty date, seek additional service, or extend the warranty, the buyer will have to pay a premium charge. In a worst case scenario, a product may have critical quality features that were not sufficiently reliability tested. If the product catastrophically fails in use and someone is hurt, then the subsequent exposure and risk would result in making the cheaper product more expensive in the long run.

At GM, effective and complete cost accounting and cost reduction systems are an important element in selecting and evaluating suppliers. Suppliers are urged to have a cost accounting system that tracks and monitors actual costs and compares them to predetermined standards. Once baselines are established, the supplier is expected to focus on reducing the cost of its product and sharing cost reductions with the customer.

An interesting point is that supplier willingness to share cost information prior to and after award of a contract is a sign of good faith in the ongoing partnership. The ultimate goal is to mutually agree on a fair price for parts and services.

COST OF QUALITY

An important element of total cost is the cost of quality (COQ). The cost of quality is the cost of doing things wrong and the cost of fixing those things. Phil Crosby, an authority on quality, believes the first step to implementing a quality partnership with a supplier is to calculate the cost of quality.

Quality costs are divided into four categories: (1) prevention, (2) appraisal, (3) internal failure, and (4) external failure. External failure, a major category, results from the poor quality of supplied materials. Customers often require the supplier to share quality cost information to determine if costs are properly distributed in terms of prevention and appraisal instead of failures. This information is also important in terms of tracking improvement and establishing goals and budgets.

COQ is especially useful for getting management's attention and increasing awareness of the importance of quality. It is estimated that 15 to 30 cents of every sales dollar in the United States is used to ensure that things are done right and to fix them if they go wrong. In contrast, Japan only spends about 5 to 10 cents of every sales dollar in this area. Japanese manufacturers therefore have a tremendous competitive cost advantage that can be used in pricing products lower to obtain marketshare.[9]

Deriving COQ numbers is not easy because they are not a part of the traditional chart of accounts or cost accounting systems. But many firms, that are becoming cost conscious and want to boost their profit margins without seeking additional sales, are focusing on reducing their cost of quality by developing realistic specifications, limiting variation around the specification target, and improving service.

Appraisal and prevention costs become significant when the failure of a nuclear safety system, artificial heart, or satellite is considered. They also become significant when the cost of lost sales due to customers' perceptions of poor quality products is considered. In terms of the competitive nature of the 1990s, many firms believe that PPM defect levels will be required to maintain customer loyalty.

USE COMMON SENSE

The selection and evaluation process discussed in this chapter requires prudence and common sense. The process is labor-intensive and time-consuming. A cost-benefit analysis should determine the products for which it should be used. It does not make sense to use this process to buy $10,000 worth of screws (unless, of course, the screws are used in applications that can affect safety or can cause an expensive malfunction).

NOTES

[1]Patrick Totty, "Service is Critical to Copier Sales Stability," *Office*, November 1988, pp. 85–86.

[2]Jonathan Wiener, "In Search of Quality Software: What Are We Really Looking For?," *Quality*, June 1988, pp. 26–30.

[3]Marlene Benmergui-Perez, "Security Every User's Responsibility," *Computing Canada*, November 10, 1988, pp. 42.

[4]Melinda Guiles and Wade Lambert, "GM Set to Cut Outside Law Firms and Rely More on In-House Staff," *Wall Street Journal*, October 30, 1989. p. B4.

[5]Richard Newman, "QFD Involves Buyers/Suppliers," *Purchasing World*, October 1988, pp. 91–93.

[6]"Can America Compete," *Time Magazine*, October 29, 1990, pp. 74–84.

[7]Richard Maass, "Supplier Certification-A Positive Response to Just in Time," *Quality Progress*, September 1988, pp. 75–80.

[8]Ford Pamphlet, "Ford Total Quality Excellence Award," 1989.

[9]Robert Goddard, "In Search of Quality," *Management World*, May/June 1988, pp. 19–21.

Chapter Eight

Partnership Building

P artnering is built on mutual trust. And partnering will only work if the trust is built upon a proven, enduring, long term, win-win relationship.

To establish and build this relationship, partnering, especially initially, should be based on the tenet of trust but verify. The verification may be a management audit, product performance test, inspection of a critical dimension, surface finish check, or customer service evaluation.

Both parties should view partnering as a long-term means to maintain and expand marketshare in existing product lines and to create new products for new markets. The customer expects to verify supplier compliance to quality standards and supplier pursuit of companywide continuous improvement. A supplier should view some form of assessment as a benign and necessary condition of being a partner.

The customer needs to verify that the supplier is truly doing what is required. Not verifying is extremely risky. The customer cannot be left in a position where an unforeseen event or problem may arise and the customer's plant may be forced to close. No customer should have to assume this risk. Furthermore, progressive suppliers understand this and view the assessment as a means to understand customer requirements and expectations which may lead to future contracts.

A periodic assessment also assures the customer that supplier wide, continuous improvement is being pursued. Continuous improvement does not happen naturally. It requires a sense of market urgency. When a supplier becomes content with its quality, service, cost, and delivery levels, these may be an early signal that there is no improvement. This is a dangerous condition in markets that change rapidly.

Suppliers to intermediate manufacturers (supplier's supplier) may be three or four tiers away from the final user. Often these suppliers have little contact with the final user and know only the immediate buyer, which in the resource chain is the immediate customer. Also, many small suppliers do not have a sense of the competitive marketplace because they do not compete directly for the final customer's attention. No contact can breed complacency and resistance to change.

SUPPLIER ASSESSMENT

A supplier is assessed throughout the certification process from candidate to partner. Once a supplier has been certified as a partner, the supplier is still periodically evaluated and monitored throughout the life of the contract. It should be mentioned that service providers are similarly monitored.

The type, extent, and duration of the assessment is determined by the criticality of the product and the level of assurance required by the client, the person or group requesting the audit. Obviously, critical, expensive, one-of-a-kind, and life maintaining products require more extensive review. The level of assurance depends on the type of information required, type of deficiency reported, costs, risks of not auditing, supplier location, and contractual requirements. Also, the customer may require a high level of compliance, such as to the Malcolm Baldrige National Quality Award criteria, discussed in Chapter 4. Obviously this type of audit or assessment is more extensive than simply analyzing the failure of a product.

There are no hard and fast rules about when an external or internal assessment should occur. A limited assessment may occur in the following situations:

- Market needs assessment.
  If the customer has developed a new product, a market and quality assessment may review the product to determine if it is safe and does what it is designed to do. Also, it determines if the product is being introduced onto the market too early.
- Product development.
  If a partner is intimately involved in product development, the partner's project plan, design, prototype, calculations, and quality systems may be reviewed. The review checks for oversights, misinterpretations, miscalculations, and associated risks. If mistakes occur and are not corrected, they may affect product function and safety.
- Design transfer.
  If a design is transferred from the partner's engineering group directly to the customer, the design may be reviewed for mistakes and checked for manufacturability and testability.
- Product modification.
  If a product is extensively modified by the partner, it may be checked as though the product was new or as if it was being transferred to manufacturing for the first time.
- Process change.
  If an in-control and capable process has been producing acceptable parts, a major process change may introduce additional process variation. The major process variables may again be examined to assure that they are in control and capable.
- New contract.
  A new contract may require the supplier to assure the customer that internal processes are capable of producing the product.

- Special product.
  A special product may be unique or expensive. Every critical quality characteristic of the product would be checked, especially if the product deals with safety or health.

UNUSUAL SITUATIONS OR CONDITIONS

There are unusual conditions or emergency situations that automatically should generate an assessment. A supplier should be assessed if any of the following occur:

- Major product failure.
  A major product failure mandates an immediate assessment by the technical and legal staff. Risks and ensuing liability exposure always should be minimized. As pharmaceutical tampering incidents have illustrated, a major product failure or incident draws media attention and demands immediate resolution.
- Customer complaints.
  A customer complaint is a premonition of an upcoming problem. A number of customer complaints may presage a major product failure.
- Chronic quality problems.
  Persistent minor quality problems can dull the luster of a product's reputation because customers will perceive that the product and the organization behind the product are no longer concerned about quality. Unfortunately, the long term result is loss of consumer confidence, which translates to loss of sales.
- Frequent shortages of material.
  A frequent shortage of material in a true Just-In-Time operation can shut down a production line.
- Late delivery of material.
  Late delivery of material also can shut down a manufacturing line unless there is some buffer stock. However, a major tenet of JIT is that all inventory should be eliminated.

- Defective material.

  A shipment of defective material requires that all future shipments be canceled until the root cause of the defect is discovered and eliminated.
- Lack of product review.

  If a supplier does not periodically review a product's function, quality, fit, manufacturability, or cost throughout product development, this indicates sloppy management and a problem waiting to occur.
- High quality costs.

  High external and internal failure costs indicate that the supplier is not investing in appraisal and prevention activities.

ASSESSMENT TECHNIQUES

There are a number of methods for assessing and monitoring suppliers. The choice of method is determined by the level of assurance the client wants and the criticality of the product. The higher the assurance, the higher the cost and time required to reach that level of assurance. Common assessment methods are:

- Certifications.

  The certification process has been discussed already. Its major advantage is that a supplier must progressively pass more difficult tests to become a single source partner.
- Surveys.

  A survey is usually a short self-assessment that a candidate or existing supplier may be asked to conduct before the customer's audit team conducts an on-site survey.
- Mechanical-chemical or similar tests.

  A mechanical test, such as a tensile test, evaluates the strength of a product. Other tests may evaluate chemical, physical, or dimensional properties.
- Reliability test.

  A reliability test measures long-term product quality. These tests duplicate conditions in which the product is used.

- First article inspection.
  The first article from a process is examined to determine if the product can be made to conform to all critical specifications.
- Incoming material inspection.
  Incoming statistical sampling and inspection at a certain quality level can verify the supplier's assertion of quality.
- Failure mode and effects analysis (FMEA).
  The major modes of failure of a product are identified and these are then eliminated, or the product is made more robust at the points of possible failure.
- Design of experiments (DOE).
  DOE is a statistical technique to identify the major factors in a process that may cause variation.
- Statistical process control.
  SPC charts indicate if a process is in control and capable of meeting specifications.
- Capability studies.
  A capability study indicates if a product can be consistently produced by a manufacturing process.
- Quality costs.
  Quality costs indicate how costs are allocated in terms of internal failure, external failure, prevention, and appraisal.
- Audits.
  Audits can be used to evaluate and monitor supplier performance. An important use of an audit is to verify if internal quality controls exist and work. An audit may use interviews, sampling data, and other tests to verify internal controls.

QUALITY AUDITING

Financial and internal auditing have been used for years and are well understood and established. Supplier quality auditing is a new development that is increasing in importance, and over time, will develop its own set of codified standards and procedures.

A quality audit is a formal and systematic assessment of suppliers. An audit serves different purposes. An audit can confirm that quality management objectives are being met, policies are being adhered to, and standards are being followed. In general, quality auditing involves the following factors:

- A process of accumulating, evaluating, and understanding evidence.
- Evidence is gathered by competent, trained, and independent people.
- Evidence can be quantitative or qualitative.
- The purpose is to determine and report on the degree of correspondence between evidence and established criteria.
- Criteria can be policies, procedures, standards, instructions, contract or test results.[1]

AUDIT STANDARDS

There are no specific standards for quality auditors like there are for certified public accountants (CPA). Various professional groups are developing voluntary standards for their implementation, which include the following:

- Auditor has adequate technical training and proficiency.
- Auditor is independent in fact and in appearance.
- Auditor exercises due professional care in conducting the audit and in preparing the audit report.
- Audit work is adequately planned and personnel are properly supervised.
- Auditor evaluates auditee's internal quality control and assurance practices, standards, and procedures.
- Auditor secures evidence through inspection, tests, observation, inquiries, or confirmations to form the basis for a reasonable opinion regarding the quality status under observation.
- Audit report states the extent to which the evidence corresponds to established criteria.
- Audit report expresses conclusions and recommendations regarding the state of quality.

- If necessary, the audit reports the necessity of corrective action on root causes with intended date of completion.[2]

INTERNAL CONTROL

Fundamental to all quality auditing is the concept of internal control. Internal control is the assurance that a quality system is in place and working properly. Examples of internal control are SPC systems, design reviews, and supplier certifications. The existence and level of internal control can determine whether an audit is required, or sometimes, if one is even possible. If the level of internal control is high, less evidence has to be gathered. If the level of internal control is low, then the auditor may have to dig deeper and gather more evidence to ensure that the quality of products and services is maintained.

Depending on the type of audit and its objectives, the level of internal control can be assessed by evaluating the following:

- Quality manual.
  A thorough quality manual indicates that the supplier has defined critical internal objectives and controls and stated how they will be implemented.
- Quality organization.
  The quality organization should be autonomous and have sufficient authority to implement corrective action and other changes.
- Training.
  Training in quality, manufacturability, and other areas requires the investment of resources and indicates an organization is committed to continuous improvement.
- Certification.
  If the supplier certifies its own suppliers, this indicates that quality through the design, procurement, production, distribution, and marketing chain is being pursued.
- Quality planning.
  Companywide quality improvement requires planning in terms of developing objectives, assigning accountabilities, and allocating resources to achieve these objectives.

- Quality information systems.
  To improve quality throughout the organization and supplier base requires that baselines are established so that improvements can be measured. Also, company-wide quality requires real-time measurement of many production process variables to determine if they are in control and capable.
- Incoming material control.
  Incoming material, meaning purchased components or raw material, should be uniform and conform to specifications.
- In process statistical controls.
  Statistical techniques should be used to prevent defects from occurring.
- Final product test and evaluation.
  Complex products are often system tested. Even if components, subassemblies, and assemblies are evaluated for quality, final product quality should be monitored because the interaction of many components may reveal problems that were not anticipated at the component level.
- Corrective action.
  Problems will occur. The manner and the time it takes to eliminate the symptom and root cause reflects the organization's efficiency and quality commitment.
- Measuring equipment and calibration.
  Measurement tools should be stored securely, handled safely, and calibrated periodically.

PROBLEMS AND THEIR RESOLUTION

Inevitably, a problem or emergency will arise, preferably during the certification process, but also may occur during the partnership. The problem may involve a contractual dispute, non-compliance, nonconforming products, late or early delivery, or poor service.

If problems arise when a supplier is a candidate partner, the manner in which the problem is resolved reflects on the future working partnership between the customer and supplier. If the problem is resolved quickly, effectively, and amicably then this bodes well for the future partnership.

A kneejerk reaction of finger pointing and blaming can destroy the new relationship. If petty problems degenerate into irreconcilable issues, then this again is an early message of how a future partnership will evolve.

Again, the first major dispute will test the new working relationship. The first dispute should be seen as an opportunity to solidify the relationship and build the trust that is essential to any future partnering. The customer and supplier should have a systematic approach to handling disputes.

In general, disputes can be resolved in any of the following ways:

- Accept.
  Accepting the problem means tabling it until it arises again, and it will. In continuous improvement, symptoms and root causes are eliminated. The next time, the result can be more damaging. Also, acceptance sends the wrong signal to the supplier that deficiencies will be tolerated.
- Negotiate.
  A problem sometimes may be negotiated away through some quid pro quo. This is not preferred unless the solution is mutually beneficial.
- Litigate.
  Litigation is the least preferred option. No one wins except the lawyers.
- Corrective action.
  Corrective action is the preferred option.

TYPES OF CORRECTIVE ACTION

Corrective action is the ability to correct the problem by eliminating the symptom and its root cause. The following is a list of ways these can be accomplished:

- Visit plant.
  A plant or supplier visit can clarify issues and resolve problems on-site. Face to face discussions are usually more effective than telephone discussions.
- Improve process.
  The customer may ask the supplier to reorganize the process or buy new machinery.
- Re-design or modify product.
  The customer or supplier may redesign the product to make it manufacturable.
- Re-modify process.
  A manufacturing process may be realigned into cells where a group of workers is responsible for all the work in an assembly.
- Train suppliers.
  Many large customers are providing quality and statistical training to suppliers.
- Update specifications.
  Specifications can be updated by loosening or developing new specifications.
- Increase incoming inspection.
  If incoming inspection is being used, then it can be increased in frequency as well as quality level. This is not a preferred course of corrective action.
- Additional monitoring.
  Monitoring the quality program, processes, or product can locate areas of deficiency that may help increase quality.

When corrective action or inducements fail to encourage change, what can be done? Several alternatives are available:

- Manufacture product in-house.
  This make or buy option is difficult or impossible late in product development. The feasibility and attractiveness of this option depends on product cost, internal and supplier capability, and availability of trained personnel, space, and equipment.

- Find new suppliers.
  This option requires time, effort, and money that usually is not feasible in the middle of a project.

WHAT IF?

I have been asked: "Does partnering require a formal agreement, such as a written contract?" Partnering commitments often result from an agreement that is secured by a handshake. This seems somewhat unconventional in a system that relies heavily on formal, legal agreements. A handshake tends to build trust and commitment more quickly than a contract. What happens if disputes arise? Often both parties agree to some form of mediation.

Sometimes the partnership does not work, usually because of poor communication and a poor understanding of mutual expectations and needs. If the relationship reaches the stage where differences cannot be reconciled, then the ultimate response is to break the relationship. This should, however, be the last recourse.

Before this occurs, the customer has several options. The preferred option, periodic auditing, should be used to review performance and explain expectations. If properly conducted, it should preclude resorting to these other options:

- Sending letter to management.
  A letter to the president of a supplier gets attention and action. The letter should state the problem, expected resolution, and a timetable.
- Initiating and increasing inspection.
  This is a temporary fix. Increased inspection sends the wrong message to the supplier. This should only be done if the situation demands it.
- Returning goods.
  Nonconforming goods can be returned to the supplier.
- Backbilling for sort and inspection.
  Backbilling for 100 percent inspection can be done if the supplier has been forewarned.

- Backbilling for rework.
  If this has been arranged with the supplier, rework may be accomplished at the customer's plant. Cost and time should be negotiated with the supplier before a problem occurs.
- Cancelling contracts.
  Cancellation is a major step that should only be used when all other alternatives have been pursued.

The next two chapters discuss how engineering, purchasing, and manufacturing are becoming more internally integrated as well as how key suppliers are incorporated into the customer's product development team.

NOTES

[1] Adapted from Alvin Arens and James Loebbecke, *Auditing: An Integrated Approach*, 2nd Ed., Englewood Cliffs: Prentice-Hall, 1980, p. 3.
[2] Ibid.

Chapter Nine
Engineering

Time is a potent weapon for improving competitiveness. U.S. companies have been leaders in inventing new processes or scientific products but have been relatively slow in introducing these products to market. U.S. companies often failed to see a product's commercial applications. And if a new product was developed, it was not improved throughout its useful life so that the product kept abreast or ahead of changing market needs.

COMPANYWIDE AND
SUPPLIERWIDE IMPROVEMENT

The process of continuous improvement is now being managed much more carefully throughout product development and the product life cycles. A new product developed and introduced quickly has a higher chance of wide acceptance before emulators come in with a cheaper or better product with more features. It is generally believed that the first product or service introduced captures up to 50 percent or more of the market-share before lower-priced emulators move in.[1] Thus, to gain a market edge, development cycle times also have been reduced from design conception to market introduction by having internal departments and key supplier-partners work together to simultaneously develop and introduce marketable products.

To accomplish this, product development is moving upstream, companywide and supplierwide. Internal and external elements are being integrated into a product development team that is responsible for designing, manufacturing, sourcing, and introducing the product to market. This development approach has some common elements that include:

- Bringing all necessary resources, including people, equipment, material, suppliers, and money together at the start of the project.
- Using small teams to guide the process through the development cycle.
- Having one group provide the critical link between each internal department involved with the product.
- Creating a multifunctional workforce.
- Integrating manufacturing and engineering into the development process by having manufacturing-engineers work with research and development engineers.[2]

Product teams may simultaneously be working at every level of a product, from assembly and subassembly to even the component level.

SIMULTANEOUS DEVELOPMENT

In the linear, discrete approach to product development, marketing determined what a customer wanted and communicated these requirements to engineering. Engineering distilled the vague customer requirements into realistic specifications and then into buildable prints. Purchasing received a bill of materials and found suppliers for components, assemblies, and factory equipment. Internal or supplier manufacturing was given a set of prints and then struggled to produce the product. Distribution moved products to the field and sales communicated product benefits to the customer.

In this linear process, was everything done correctly the first time? No. Manufacturing or suppliers often kicked prints back to engineering and requested more information. Approvals flowed upward and then downward. Decisions sometimes didn't get made. Problems were accepted and became chronic.

Extensive revisions would start the whole process again. Or an engineering design or calculation error could stop everything until an engineering change order was made and the process started over again. In general, communication and coordination were poor.

The problem was that the development of a marketable product took a long time. Eventually, managers established departmental bureaucracies with the seeming mission of protecting their turfs. Departments with special expertise and knowledge that should have been consulted were not. And once a product was developed, it sometimes had to be redesigned because it did not satisfy a market niche.

ENGINEERING INTEGRATION

The tendency of engineering to become more specialized exacerbated the problem. Specialization created people who were expert in their disciplines but poor in terms of coordinating and communicating with others who should have been consulted.

Experts in industrial design, product engineering, and manufacturing engineering often would not communicate with each other during product development. Traditionally, industrial design was responsible for conceptual and external design including aesthetics, packaging, styling, decoration, and logos. Product engineering took conceptual designs and developed drawings and realistic product specifications. Manufacturing-engineering converted product designs into detailed drawings suitable for production. Since each area was perceived as being discrete, it was difficult to translate designs into production prints and then into products that satisfied a market niche.

The urgency of exceeding customer's fickle expectations now requires the seamless integration of engineering subdisciplines, organizational functional areas, and key supplier-partners. The hope is that coordination among all parties will result in an appealing, robust design that ultimately benefits the final customer, manufacturer, and supplier-partner.

CUSTOMER AND SUPPLIER INTEGRATION

Just as engineers cannot throw a complex design to manufacturing and expect a design to be built to specifications, the customer cannot throw a complex modification or new product design to any supplier and expect the modification or product to be built to specifications.

Poor design affects every product. Parts may be designed with features that are difficult to fabricate, with tolerances that are unnecessarily tight. Or incomplete or loose tolerances may cause parts to conflict with other parts. The solution is to integrate key supplier-partners with manufacturing expertise and design knowledge into the customer's product development team.

Quality levels have increased. Delivery schedules are within tighter windows and service has become generally polite and expeditious. Design and research capabilities are becoming more important too. New products are designed and introduced quickly. They are more technical and electronic. Customers necessarily must rely on their world-class supplier-partners for specific expertise in developing, designing, and manufacturing a higher order product or assembly instead of simply providing components.

Customer expectations of a supplier's technical capability have increased tremendously in recent years. The supplier-partner is expected to:

- Design and develop aesthetic, maintainable, and reliable products.
- Use advanced computer-aided equipment to design, test, and simulate product use.
- Dedicate in-house resources to research, design, and develop new products.
- Simplify products.

- Use customer feedback to improve products.
- Continuously update products throughout the product life cycle.
- Identify and eliminate a product's weak points.
- Have the capability to perform performance tests on parts and systems.
- Have resources to implement prototype part development.
- Be aware of liability and have processes to control it.
- Ensure that contractors have similar technical capabilities.

Recently, an automotive manufacturer wanted to reengineer every major element of its product to improve its quality and economy. Customer engineers asked one supplier with specific product expertise to solve several of their engineering problems. Supplier engineers worked with the customer's engineers to reduce the number of internal parts by standardizing products. The supplier also had to control and improve its internal manufacturing processes. The win for the customer was overall product consolidation, significant costs savings, increased quality, and increased product value. The win for the supplier was long-term business with guaranteed margins.

IS IT WORKING?

Again, the future can be glimpsed in the automotive industry and its suppliers as they face increased competition from Japanese transplants. To remain competitive, the auto companies and suppliers are partnering to match, and with some notable successes, to surpass the Japanese transplants in product quality and in reducing product cycle times. Chrysler Corp., which is especially feeling market pressures, has a corporate mandate to cut its new car development cycle in half.[3] Fortune magazine recently reported that the multidisciplinary team approach to simultaneous development and improvement reduced product introduction cycle times in many U.S. companies by as much as 50 to 70 percent.

Simultaneous engineering and development are also working in other industries. NCR Corporation successfully used simultaneous engineering to improve its terminals at supermarket checkout counters. The new counter was brought on the market in 22 months, half the normal time used to develop the previous product. The new product had 85 percent fewer parts than the previous model and could be assembled in two minutes, or one-fourth the time it normally took. The message was heard. Engineering, design, purchasing, and field support specialists are now in the same area, working together to exchange information throughout product development.[4]

For years, Digital Equipment Corporation (DEC) secured a market edge by continuously updating its computers. DEC's VAX has become the longest used major computer line in industry by covering a wide performance range. Since the design of the first VAX, the 780, VAX architecture has been updated more than 12 times.[5]

DESIGNING FOR MANUFACTURABILITY, RELIABILITY, AND MAINTAINABILITY

Authorities on quality believe that poor design contributes up to 40 percent of all quality problems.[6] So, the search for quality starts by emphasizing accurate, precise, realistic, and attainable specifications that reflect the quality characteristics which satisfy a customer need. Otherwise, an engineering miscalculation or design flaw will be replicated in each product.

There are few universal guidelines for good design. One rule, however, that seems to remain constant with the increasing complexity of products, is the KISS principle, Keep It Sweet and Simple. Complex designs lead to excessive tooling, material manufacturing, and processing costs. Also, potential problems have to be anticipated during design because there is little time or it is too expensive to modify a product late in the product development cycle. It is equally difficult and expensive to remedy mistakes once it is on the market. In addition, complexity can dramatically lower manufacturability, reliability, and maintainability.

DESIGN FOR MANUFACTURABILITY

Early in the development process, the product development team determines how a new product will be produced and which components will be made internally or purchased. This process is commonly called design for manufacturability (DFM).

The team tries to establish design requirements that transfer designs from the design computer to production by considering and optimizing all possible design elements, so that iterations due to changes, approvals, redesign, or expediting are minimized. This process becomes complex as the development team tries to optimize many factors such as process costs, operator training, standard materials, material flow, ease of assembly, availability of machines, and production layout for fabrication, assembly, and testing.

The goal is to design it right the first time and thereby reduce the iterations and mistakes that have plagued design in the past. In terms of statistical thinking, this can be seen as another effort to reduce unwanted variation in the design process.

DFM is becoming increasingly difficult as components become more complex and customized for an application. As well, the customer must rely on the partner with the specialized knowledge to design these components.

Surface mount technology (SMT) illustrates this problem. It is commonly used in electronics manufacturing because it increases the density of electronic components on a printed circuit board. One of the criteria the team must consider is how on-line equipment will access and test the circuits during production.[7]

There is no established method for designing for manufacturability. At AT&T Bell Laboratories, development teams follow this DFM systematic procedure, which has elements common to many other DFM systems:

- Establish a joint design and manufacturing team.
- Define design requirements in terms of existing or new production processes and machines.

- Evaluate cost, schedule, and quality issues of each process.
- Establish design rules based on the manufacturing processes chosen.
- Set up formal design reviews at each step of the design process from concept, design, and prototype to manufacturing engineering.
- Determine which elements of the design should be verified, whether by simulation, emulation, or model building.
- Construct a model shop prototype to anticipate future production difficulties.[8]

DESIGNING FOR RELIABILITY

Reliability is long term quality. Reliability is especially important with products, systems, or projects involving safety, health, or defense issues. No one wants a recurrence of the Three Mile Island nuclear disaster, a faulty artificial heart, or a Challenger space shuttle disaster.

Originally, the definition of quality was conformance to specifications at one point in time. If a product had a dimension that was in the middle of the specification, then it was considered acceptable. Using this static definition of quality, if the manufacturing process was in control and capable of meeting specifications, it was generally thought that defects could be prevented and product quality could be secured.

But what would happen when the product was in the hands of the customer? Would it continue operating in different environments or would it be used in unintended ways? Would preventive maintenance extend its useful life? If it failed, would it fail catastrophically? If it failed, how long and what would make it operational?

Manufacturers of critical products are concerned about these issues. For example, a pacemaker manufacturer devotes most of its human resources to reliability testing. The company spends more time testing its hybrid designs than producing them. With this product, there is especially no room for error with components purchased from suppliers. All operators, materials, processes, and tests must meet or exceed stringent company and industry specifications. All employees undergo annual written and on-the-job recertification tests. Quality assurance audits critical manufacturing operations, such as wire bonding and seam welding. And each pacemaker has documentation that describes what occurred at each manufacturing step.[9]

DESIGNING FOR MAINTAINABILITY

Designing for maintainability is important in military, commercial, and consumer products. Sophisticated military systems must be maintained and repaired in battle conditions by people who may or may not have finished high school. Commercial products, such as copiers, have built-in diagnostics, synthesized voices, or even video display that tell the customer what is wrong and how to fix the problem.

In the near future, GE believes that most new homes will have televisions that can be used to program household products or display diagnostic messages from broken equipment. A dishwasher will be able to inform the homeowner that it does not work because the door is jammed or even instruct the hot water system to increase the temperature. The television and a voice recognition system will be able to reprogram equipment such as turning lights on or off. Again, technology is becoming more friendly. Its purpose is to give the customer more control over his or her environment.

TOOLS FOR GOOD DESIGN

Computers are integral to all stages of the development process. Engineers use computer-aided-design (CAD) to reduce development cycle times and promote simultaneous engineering and manufacturing. Sophisticated design software can generate an image of a part, rotate it, simulate different operating conditions, and calculate stresses.

In state of the art facilities, customer and supplier engineering departments can electronically exchange designs, bills of material, and specifications. The advantages are many. Preproduction costs and the time to market are reduced. A major attraction of current CAD systems is that they facilitate communication and coordination through their ability to share data with other computers in an integrated design, manufacturing, inspection, and supplier network.

Suppliers are also expected to use advanced computer techniques to design and analyze new products and prototypes. Prototype development is especially important as product development times are reduced. Prototypes reveal to the customer and supplier if a product can be built and produced as shown on the print.

STRATEGIC DESIGN

The vigilant organization realizes there are many factors other than quality that may affect the buy decision. For example, in buying an automobile, the customer may care about cost, comfort, safety, gas consumption, performance, maintainability, reliability, warranty, dealer service, and product styling.

Quality and service may have provided a temporary advantage that attracted customers at one time. As cost competitive quality and service have become universally high, styling and aesthetics have become increasingly important.

DESIGN QUALITY IN THE 1980s

In the 1980s, a number of notable products separated the innovative companies from the me-too product world. These notable products were not only aesthetic, but also highly profitable for the companies. Ford Motor Co.'s Taurus, the first aero jellybean, was an instant success that propelled Ford Motor Co.'s profitability ahead of much larger GM. Apple's Macintosh computer epitomized the concept of user friendly. Apple's computers were neither the fastest nor the cheapest. Instead, Apple very carefully developed, nurtured, and communicated to its customers an image of simplicity, ease of use, and reliability.

Macintosh designers saw the machine as a work of art and everything from packaging and logo to product literature communicated this message.

It now seems that every advertisement shouts quality. Whether the ads are real or just puffery remains to be seen. All companies now seem to compete through quality. The competitive bar has been raised internally as well as among suppliers. The result is that entire markets are becoming saturated with uniformly high-quality products—those that are safe, reliable, maintainable, and conform to specifications. Furthermore, companies are matching high-quality products with high-quality services.

PLANNED OBSOLESCENCE

I once asked an eminent designer, "How do you recognize a well designed product?" After a little thought, the designer responded half seriously and half jokingly: "The product shouts use me, use me."

This concept drives linear thinking engineers crazy! How does an engineer develop prints and specifications for a product that is fun to use? If one can develop these specifications, will they be such that the product cannot be built?

Strategic design is inherently people design. It is counterintuitive and often counter-technology. For years, technology and external features were in. Digital readouts and lights covered the exterior of many products. A consumer product often looked like the cockpit of a 747. Were the dials and gauges functional? Did they tell the customer what she or he wanted to know? Often not. Also, a user's (note *not* customer's) manual detailed how to interpret the gauges and use the machine. Now, the competitive game emphasizes fun and product simplicity.

If product and service quality are uniformly high, how will companies differentiate themselves from the rest of the herd? What occurs in Japan again offers a glimpse at what may occur in the United States and in the rest of the global market.

Japanese consumers have been offered high-quality products and services for a number of years. Almost every Japanese market segment is saturated with quality products. Quality service is also legendary. Pampered and finicky Japanese customers have a dozen or more quality-brand products to choose from, but they are less interested in function and reliability than they are in the fun of using the product. Japanese consumer product manufacturers focus on a customer's total experience with a product rather than just its quality, price, or service.

Strategic design can do this. Good design makes a product robust, reliable, safe, and easily manufacturable. Strategic design creates a product and maybe more—an experience that makes the product fun to use. Strategic design emphasizes not only the interior and exterior but also the aura surrounding the product. The product should shout "use me, use me", because fun products are bought and used. So, that quality at the cutting edge of competitiveness will focus on the most abstract element of a product, its fun quotient.

Many Japanese, European, and American engineers already are doing this. Sporty automobiles are designed with throaty sounding exhaust systems. Cameras have soft curves. Radios come in the shape of an ear, are multi-colored, and have big dials. The designers try to graft a soft function onto the hard consumer product.[10]

Is there a down side to this? Yes. Unfortunately, the search for continuous novelty results in rapid product obsolescence and disposal of functional products which may create larger environmental concerns in the future.

LIABILITY CONTROL

During the last 10 years, the number of lawsuits against manufacturers has increased dramatically, largely because the liability law has been interpreted in a broad manner. Under this broad interpretation, the designer or manufacturer may be held liable if the product is defective in design, manufacture, or use.

Also, an engineer may be held personally accountable for a design defect. So, engineers are especially encouraged to design products defensively, considering all regulations, labels, and packages, as well as designing for manufacturability, reliability, and maintainability.

Designers are advised to anticipate bizarre or unexpected product uses because people injured by misusing a product have successfully sued the manufacturer. With so much of a product's value being provided by single source suppliers, they are encouraged to control exposure to liability by:

- Having a companywide quality program that emphasizes designing and building quality into the product.
- Designing redundancy and backup systems into products.
- Identifying customer complaints with feedback to the organization to incorporate the changes.
- Having a lawyer check for potential legal problems and ensure that products meet safety standards.
- Documenting the process of defensive design.
- Developing specific engineering and manufacturing standards.
- Anticipating possible loss exposures and proactively designing flaws out.

The urgency to control liability has brought legal staff into the development team. At GM, legal staff works with technical people to prevent litigation. GM lawyers work with engineers to develop more uniform welding procedures, both to enhance durability and to lower exposure to catastrophic failure. In addition, GM lawyers monitor legal suits to help engineers and suppliers pinpoint the principal causes of failure.[11]

CUSTOMER FEEDBACK

To keep existing designs current and safe, a supplier-partner is expected to pay special attention to customer surveys, field failures, and product recalls. If a customer survey elicits suggestions for improved performance or enhanced appearance, the supplier is expected to modify the product. If a product fails in the hands of the customer, the supplier must have the ability to test and evaluate the failure and eliminate the root cause. If the product has been recalled due to the failure of the supplied part, the supplier is also expected to immediately determine the root cause, eliminate it, and sometimes defray the cost of the recall.

BEST PRACTICES

Consumer product legislation is placing growing pressure on manufacturers to show that the best design practices have been used to minimize the risk of system failure. Design assurance is a structured and disciplined approach to verify design and development activities. A design-assurance program involves:

1. Defining design requirements.
2. Controlling changes in specifications and drawings.
3. Securing necessary approvals.
4. Testing designs.
5. Verifying the adequacy of designs.
6. Checking calculations.
7. Verifying customer requirements.[12]

AT&T Bell Laboratories uses a formal procedure called quality design reviews (QDRs). QDRs are an objective evaluation of a project's quality system, specifically focusing on developing realistic standards, methods, and procedures. A QDR is conducted by a team of experts in quality systems and product development. The team determines the adequacy and application of existing quality systems to develop a high quality product and to deliver it on time and on budget.[13]

The next chapter discusses the increasingly close integration of engineering and manufacturing.

NOTES

[1] James Duffy, "United Front is Faster," *Management Today,* November 1989, pp. 131–139.

[2] Nhora Cortes-Comerer, "Organizing the Design Team," *IEEE Spectrum,* May 1987, pp. 41–46.

[3] Gary Vasilash, "The American Manufacturing Challenge: Being Like the Tortoise—And the Hare," *Production*, December 1989, pp. 54–61.

[4] "A Smarter Way to Manufacture," *Business Week*, April 30, 1990, pp. 110–117.

[5] Robert Davidson, "On Good Design: Defining the Product," *IEEE Spectrum*, May 1987, pp. 29–32.

[6] Ernest Raia, "Quality in Design," *Purchasing*, April 6, 1985, pp. 58–65.

[7] Gadi Kaplan, "Designing for Producibility," *IEEE Spectrum*, May 1987, pp. 47–54.

[8] "Quality by Design," AT&T Bell Laboratories, 1986, pp. 163–164.

[9] "Seeking Ultimate Reliability," *Quality*, January 1977, pp. 54–57.

[10] Bob Johnson, "Far Eastern Economic Review," digested in *World Press Review*, May 1990, p. 63.

[11] Melinda Guiles, "GM Set to Cut Outside Law Firms and Rely More on In-House Staff," *Wall Street Journal*, October 30, 1989, p. B4.

[12] John Burgess, "Design Assurance: A Tool for Excellence," *Engineering Management International*, April 1988, pp, 25–30.

[13] AT&T Bell Laboratories, "Quality by Design," AT&T, 1986, pp. 66–67.

Chapter Ten
Manufacturing

M anufacturing excellence has been widely touted as the means to become globally competitive. What is manufacturing excellence? The manufacturing excellence philosophy integrates new manufacturing technologies and new management thinking.

New manufacturing technologies include many different elements such as computer-aided-design (CAD), computer-aided-manufacturing (CAM), robotics, computer integrated manufacturing (CIM), and flexible manufacturing systems (FMS). New management thinking is also called Just-In-Time (JIT), Total Quality Management, and Total Quality Excellence. The new philosophies emphasize attention to detail, continuous improvement, elimination of all types of waste, customer service, integration of discrete functional areas, and integration of supplier-partners.

MARKET OF ONE

Traditionally, a plant produced a large number of products that were sold in different markets. If a market niche was targeted, then special features were added to the basic product model. The basic product or model was not changed.

In the near future, the individual with his or her special requirements may be the ultimate customer. Products will be specially tailored to the needs of an ever smaller customer group, until conceivably, each customer will be able to order a product directly from the manufacturer. This will require:

- Flexible production machinery that can be adjusted quickly to satisfy special customer needs.
- Precise production monitoring.
- Process control of many product variables.
- Smooth material and information flows.

This is more than a novelty. Already customers can buy products through television, as they say, from the comfort of their home. In the future customer requirements and product specifications will be communicated directly to the factory, which will produce the products and deliver them directly to the customer.

Certain publications are already adjusting their advertising and editorial product mix in the same magazine to fit the needs of a targeted reader group. Recently, each of the nine million people who subscribed to *Time*, *People*, and *Sports Illustrated* were sent an Isuzu advertisement with their names printed on the insert card. *Time* magazine is offering ad pages that will be sent to specific readers, those who have moved recently who are over the age of 50 with high incomes, or who frequently buy products through the mail.[1]

MINIMIZING VARIATION

The integration of engineering and manufacturing is creating a synergy that previously did not exist. Traditionally, engineering design dictated production parameters. Engineering would develop specifications and drawings that manufacturing used to produce the part. The result was often chaos.

Now, the intrinsic advantages and limitations of the manufacturing process are used to develop product specifications. If a process is not in statistical control and not capable of meeting specifications, the design is either modified or the process is changed, so that both conditions are met. For example, through the purchase of new machinery, a process can be established that is capable of making the product. This is especially critical in electronic manufacturing, where engineering is continuously miniaturizing components so that they are becoming progressively more difficult to assemble and test.

The necessity to increase yields is refocusing attention to manufacturing and emphasizing an understanding of the capabilities of the production processes. For example, the following list of items is normally considered by the design team prior to pushing a design to manufacturing:

- Customer requirements are translated into product specifications.
- Product is understood.
- Process analysis determines whether a part or assembly can be produced.
- Significant elements producing variation are identified.
- Operating personnel are trained.
- Corrective action guidelines are established.
- New quality improvement opportunities are identified.
- Continuous improvement is pursued.[2]

KISS PRINCIPLE IN MANUFACTURING

To facilitate the transfer of a design from engineering to internal production or to a partner's production facility, the Keep it Sweet and Simple (KISS) principle can be used again. To simplify design and manufacturing, several KISS design and manufacturing basics are kept in mind, such as:

- Eliminate unnecessary steps.
- Simplify all production processes.
- Group similar parts into a single product.
- Separate manual from mechanical operations.
- Reduce the number of components.
- Standardize designs.

A major issue confronting many companies is finding the right balance between producing a product in-house and encouraging supplier-partners to produce the product. More and more technology content is in components. More often, a customer designs, assembles, and tests a final product. Key supplier/partners develop components and assemblies which require that they have advanced research, design, and production facilities. Who pays for these? It is common for the customer to invest in the supplier-partner to develop custom-designed components for the customer to assemble.

In general, a product with fewer parts has higher reliability, can be assembled faster and cheaper, and results in lower operational costs. For example, one supplier had an imaginative idea to provide a modular door to an automotive customer. The automobile door consisted of 100 or more mechanical and electronic parts, which had come from dozens of suppliers. The parts were then assembled in the customer's facility. This took time and required additional resources. This added complexity to the customer's facility. By working with a key supplier-partner that supplied the modular door, the number of parts was cut down to 13 and the supplier to one.[3]

Accompanying this trend of modular sourcing is the trend of shifting more responsibilities onto the supplier. One high-tech organization conducts only research and development (R&D) and final testing in-house. Approximately 90 percent of this firm's manufacturing dollar is out-sourced, including all manufacturing, purchasing, and assembling. The only internal operations after a purchase order has been cut are testing, packaging, and shipping the product.

MANUFACTURING TECHNOLOGY

Once the variation of a specific process is understood and a culture of continuous improvement has been established, only then should an organization think about automating the factory. This was different several years ago when a factory would be automated without understanding the implications of poor supplied parts, inadequate trained workforce, and recalcitrant first level supervision.

COMPUTER INTEGRATED MANUFACTURING

The future plant will consist of integrated design and production machinery. This arrangement sometimes is called computer integrated manufacturing (CIM). CIM is not so much based on managing individual production machinery, but rather on grouping resources, including human, material, information, and machinery, into an integrated system.

In advanced CIM facilities, computers communicate with each other, transferring information from marketing to engineering to production machinery. In these plants, computer-aided design (CAD), computer-aided manufacturing (CAM), robotics, computer-numerically controlled (CNC) machinery, flexible manufacturing systems (FMS), automated storage and retrieval systems, and automated inspection share critical information. Key supplier-partners are integrated into this information loop. Computer-generated designs and bills of material can be sent electronically to production machinery and inspection equipment.

Computer-integrated manufacturing helps a company to meet different needs quickly, bring new ideas to commercialization speedily, reduce information costs through data interchange, and bring customers and suppliers much closer together in terms of understanding each other's needs and satisfying specifications consistently.[4]

Another advantage is that CIM robots are flexible. They can be programmed for different operations. In auto plants, robots can be programmed to machine piece parts, assemble intricate components, paint auto panels, and inspect finished products.

GM's plant in Lansing, Michigan, produces the high-quality Quad 4 engine. GM wanted to produce 100 percent defect-free engines at production capacity. There was no provision for repair or reworking in machining. Operators were given control and responsibility of the processes. Tedious, time-consuming, and dangerous processes were automated. Continuous automated monitoring equipment constantly monitored major process variables so that if a nonconformance was about to occur, it was corrected before parts were rejected.[5]

MANUFACTURING AUTOMATION

A Flexible Manufacturing System (FMS) is a machine or a set of machines that are capable of performing different operations with great precision on a variety of parts in a random job sequence. So, if a customer or a group of customers wants a product with specific characteristics, those products can be easily produced in small runs.

Managing a complex manufacturing process constitutes a major control problem that FMS machinery can help alleviate. In some plants, each product is measured during the manufacturing process and necessary corrective action is automatically undertaken before the next piece is produced. So, if a particular machine is subject to out of control shifts and possibly shifts out of the specification limits, a feedback loop automatically adjusts the machine.

A product may have 100 or more critical quality dimensional characteristics. How does a supplier monitor this many? Obviously, manual monitoring is impractical. An automated process can track, monitor, and control many variables simultaneously.

Highly automated machines use real-time SPC software to track the quality characteristics. To control this diverse and distributed environment, a number of intelligent devices are connected in a network to gather and analyze data that controls individual operations. These devices can gather, analyze, and distribute quality data, sometimes directly from the supplier's manufacturing process to the customer's engineering organization.

One hundred percent inspection may become more feasible with on-line SPC and automatic test equipment. One switch manufacturer used SPC in conjunction with 100 percent robotic testing equipment to reduce the number of product defects. An automatic tester was built to test each switch for electrical continuity and actuation force. If a defect was detected, a robotic arm picked up the defective switch and placed it in a reject box. The goal to reduce defects to a parts per million defect (PPM) level was achieved. The defect rate was reduced from 11,000 PPM to 100 PPM with corresponding savings.[6]

At another plant, testing became a bottleneck on the production line. Material that had to be removed and tested brought production to a standstill. This is no longer the case. On-line high-speed hardness testing is now possible because automated material-handling systems can move, clamp, test, and release a part, frequently in less than a second.[7]

IT'S A SLOW PROCESS

A recent survey revealed half of the companies that had invested in automation were getting negative or low payoffs. Many automated applications failed due to not understanding the manufacturing environment and poor product designs. Advanced integrated manufacturing technologies should be seen in the context of the entire organization, instead of discrete pieces of production machinery. A successful CIM application requires a thorough understanding of the process being automated and how it will be integrated into the communication and resource networks.

JUST-IN-TIME

Delivery of material now means more than dropping material onto a loading dock. Proper delivery means that the supplier understands customer packaging, labeling, handling, and shipping requirements. Proper packaging ensures that products are delivered safely. Proper labeling, often bar coded, identifies part name, quantities, pack date, engineering print, and name of supplier. Proper handling ensures that parts are not inadvertently abused. Proper shipping ensures that parts are delivered intact.

Also, proper delivery means that material is delivered to specific locations within tight time windows. These delivery time windows may change with little notice, so a supplier must be able to adjust volumes and schedules to accommodate the customer.

Several years ago, JIT delivery was defined in terms of a day's window. Now, JIT delivery is within hours and within a prescribed sequence. Sequenced delivery is common to automotive plants, where supplied parts are unloaded in a predetermined sequence and ready to be assembled onto a specific automobile. To illustrate, seats that are black, blue, red, and then black may be unloaded from a truck to be immediately assembled onto black, blue, red, and black automobiles. If the sequence is not in the same order as the assembly line, resources are wasted in matching colored seats to the automobile color.

To improve the integration of the supplier with the customer's requirements, communication between the customer and supplier-partner must be accurate and timely. To ensure this, the data—whether purchase orders, shipping schedules, engineering prints, or specifications—are transferred electronically.

JIT AS MANAGEMENT ETHIC

Just-In-Time delivery has evolved into a management ethic of manufacturing excellence. The new wave of manufacturing management spreading throughout the world originated in Japan and is usually linked to Just-In-Time (JIT). JIT was first identified with minimum or zero inventory levels. This narrow interpretation, however, hindered its development.

Many companies later adopted the Toyota JIT system, which can generally be characterized as a means to eliminate all types of waste. Wastes include: overproduction, excessive inventory, unnecessary handling, unnecessary processes, waiting time, wasted motions by production operators, and product defects.[8]

Waste elimination requires a broader interpretation of JIT. It was quickly discovered that JIT could not be a stand-alone program. JIT evolved into an approach of management excellence blending high quality, low cost, flexibility, delivery, and dependability. JIT became associated with the never ending commitment to company and supplier wide continuous improvement. So, continuous improvement now also implies reducing inventory while increasing the dependence on a narrower supplier base.

INTERNAL JIT

JIT is sometimes called demand-pull manufacturing. JIT is based on pulling parts through the assembly line upon receiving a customer order. Each pull creates a vacuum in the preceding stage so that additional units are manufactured to replace the pulled parts. At the ideal, production becomes a single conduit with a smooth work flow. The focus is on designing manufacturing areas into networks that help parts and assemblies move smoothly, with minimum movement of the partially completed product.

The object of internal JIT is to produce a minimum lot size, so that an item can be immediately used by the next work station thereby eliminating buffer inventory. Flexibility provided by CIM systems facilitates this.

In true JIT, there is little room for error. If material builds up, the production line is no longer smooth, and the process will go back to a stop and start operation. Also, poor quality material from a supplier will force the production line to stop. A major advantage to JIT is that it draws attention to problems and mistakes if the system is not working properly, thus enabling corrective action to be taken.

EXTERNAL JIT

In optimum JIT, a customer sale generates an order that starts the process of pulling products from the production line. The customer's final assembly line schedule triggers the withdrawal of the exact number of parts needed. In JIT, order levels should be stabilized with sufficient lead times so that the supplier can match and balance processes to accommodate the customer. This means that if the customer's manufacturing line slows down, the same occurs with the supplier's line. Theoretically, the supplier's last operation is synchronized with the customer's first operation that uses the product.

Communication links between customer and supplier must necessarily be close. Having multiple suppliers of the same product causes confusion. Again, JIT encourages partnering because to operate successfully, JIT requires fewer suppliers, long-term contracts, small lot sizes, and very high-quality material. To do this, customers encourage world-class supplier-partners to adopt similar focused factory arrangements that emphasize a limited number of products or processes.

This also changes purchasing's role from placing orders to managing and monitoring a supplier's management, technical, and process capabilities. Again, the assumption is that if these exist and are operating properly, product quality can be assured and continuous improvement pursued.

RIGHT NEXT DOOR

JIT also favors domestic suppliers because it is much easier to adjust one's operations if a partner is located nearby. When determining the site of assembly plants, the location of key suppliers is critical for Japanese transplants. With over 75 percent of Honda's suppliers within a 150-mile radius of the Marysville, Ohio, assembly plant, most parts on the production line are delivered daily to the Honda assembly plant within tight delivery windows.

Similarly, Molex built a factory in Huntsville, Alabama, to supply Chrysler Corp.'s Acustar Inc. with defect-free electrical components and connector assemblies for radios, and electronic instruments, within three and a half hours of receiving a computerized order. This plant, located close to the customer, is a prototype of many plants gearing up for Just-In-Time manufacturing and delivery. At first, delivery to the customer is supported by a buffer stock of inventory. As production flows smooth out, the inventory is gradually removed, so that true JIT manufacturing can occur.[9]

While it may not be possible for a JIT supplier to locate near the customer's plant, JIT can still work if customer demand is known or can be accurately projected so that the supplier is given a stable schedule.

JIT also requires a stable transportation delivery system. A supplier may be expected to deliver loads two or more times a day. Stability is ensured by jointly planning delivery windows and prescribing truck routes. Carriers often go through the same qualification process as product or service suppliers.

JIT CHALLENGES

JIT seems too good to be true. Inventories, leadtime, costs and paperwork are all reduced. Quality is increased. The number of firms that use JIT is small, however. According to one estimate, 40 percent or fewer firms use some form of JIT. This is amazing if one realizes that 30 percent or more of a business's assets can be tied up in some form of inventory.

Probably, the main reason why JIT is not more widespread is because it is not easy. Quality of supplied material must be very high, preferably in terms of parts per million defect rate. The customer and supplier must communicate and coordinate schedules and demands. The ability to produce in small lots to meet a customer's workstation requirements or send materials at the right time, at the right quantity to the exact location are management and organizational issues as much as anything else.

Through proper planning, training, and a commitment to share decision making, JIT can be developed. Teamwork, mutual trust, and open communications to develop solutions and prevent recurring problems are all required.

Sometimes, suppliers are reluctant to get involved in JIT. Suppliers perceive that they are being asked to shoulder burdens of more frequent deliveries and improved quality levels while not being offered assistance or inducements to achieve these goals. JIT can be coupled with a continuous improvement effort and can be sold to suppliers and made attractive through the same inducements discussed earlier.

CAVEAT

According to surveys, Japanese factories seem to outperform those in the United States. U.S. manufacturers are applying

Japanese techniques haphazardly in factories, not thinking about the implications of their use. The list is long and includes quality circles, kaizen, Just-In-Time, quick change machine dies, and so on.

Basic economic and social differences between Japan and the West make it impractical to adopt Japanese practices wholesale without adapting them. Caution and patience must be exercised. Modular product design, widespread automation, participatory management, high group morale, and widespread training evolved gradually in Japanese factories. Grafting a particular new philosophy, machine, or technique is a quick fix solution and a prescription for failure.

TRAINING

In the 1980s, every organization invested in technology, believing it was the key to improved quality, lowered costs, and purchasing effectiveness. This proved to be a false assumption. Technology is not a substitute for good management.

Change in manufacturing will not occur unless there is a radical change in mindset to be flexible, to adapt to changing market conditions, to focus on the customer, and to improve continuously. Flexibility must also be balanced by the need to be self-disciplined. Self-discipline is required because variation in every operation must be monitored and controlled through statistically-driven prevention.

Also, technology will not be used if it is beyond the abilities of people to understand, use, and manage it. Furthermore, it won't be used unless the people in middle management who direct its use are induced to change, take risks, and adopt new methods. Middle management has been known to be threatened by the use of technology and to covertly stymie new development.

Again, the Auto Industry

During the last several years, the auto industry learned some valuable and painful lessons on how to compete in a global economy. One important lesson confirmed that technology is just a tool and that more data do not translate into increased managerial effectiveness.

GM bought Electronic Data Systems to computerize its factories. It also bought Hughes Aircraft to bring high-tech aerospace design to automobile design and manufacturing. GM discovered in its drive to be the industry's technology leader that technology is always dependent on people who use it. A company must involve its people in technological changes through continuous training that is tailored to them and the process in which they work. Inevitably, technologies must fit into the skill set of the worker.

Since technology is only part of the answer, companies are training people and pushing responsibility for quality down to the organization. This means that the person responsible for a task, whether it is the assembly person on the line, the engineer designing piece parts, the supervisor managing a work area, or the buyer purchasing products, is being trained. Similarly, suppliers are extensively trained in quality. The purpose is to place decisions at the appropriate operating level and promote experimentation and risk taking.

Both elements of excellence require a change in philosophy, culture, and even organizational structure. Specifically, the requirements are a flat organizational structure, cost-accounting systems measuring quality costs, performance-based compensation systems, and management of workers with different ethnic and cultural backgrounds.

NOTES

[1]David Jacobson, "Magazines Increasingly Become Customized," *Oregonian*, January 7, 1990, p. D4.

[2]Joseph Tunner, "Total Manufacturing Process Control - The High Road to Product Control," *Quality Progress*, October 1987, pp. 43–50.

[3]Ernest Raia, "JIT in Detroit," *Purchasing Magazine*, September 15, 1987, pp. 72–73.

[4]Don Garvin, "Manufacturing Flexibility in the CAM Era," *Business Horizons*, Jan/Feb 1989, pp. 78–84.

[5]Robert Huber, "Automatic Assembly Tackles the Quality Issue," *Production*, July 1989, pp. 47–50.

[6]Elisabeth BenDaniel, "Using Statistical Process Control with Robotic Testing Improves Quality Level," *Industrial Engineering*, February 1988, pp. 26–31.

[7]K. J. Law, "Advanced Hardness Testing," *Quality*, May 1988, pp. 29–32.

[8]Anthony Lynch, "Managing the Product Development Process: Eliminating Waste in the Office," *Quality*, August 1989, pp. 29–30.

[9]Brian Moskal, "Automotive: Never Say 'Perfect'," *Industry Week*, February 20, 1989, pp. 35–38.

Chapter Eleven

Opportunities and Risks

M any companies once had a standard policy to buy American. As the quality of American goods and services deteriorated and costs increased, these firms engaged in offshore sourcing and manufacturing.

The Pacific Rim especially offered many attractively priced, high-quality sourcing alternatives. For example, Singapore offered technical expertise and disciplined labor. Hong Kong produced excellent quality goods in an economy that was largely entrepreneurial. The Republic of Korea had large trading corporations and large, modern, manufacturing facilities. Taiwan had thousands of small, locally owned firms that could accept low-volume orders at competitive prices.[1]

Particularly, overseas sourcing made sense if a product was proprietary; if the supplier had special knowledge, skills or resources unavailable domestically; or if domestic suppliers could not consistently meet high quality levels.

BACK IN THE UNITED STATES

While multinational companies are still designing, sourcing, producing, marketing, and distributing around the world, the pendulum is swinging back to the middle. To satisfy local market requirements and be able to adapt quickly, manufacturers who had been producing or sourcing abroad for domestic consumption, are coming back to the United States to make or buy many of their products. This is based on good business sense rather than on patriotism.

A major inducement for international purchasing was that labor costs were lower in many less-developed countries and quality was inconsequential. The percentage of labor cost to total product cost is now decreasing, however, due to automation and the high cost of product research and development. Furthermore, many developing countries don't have the resources to invest in the new technologies, processes, and product development that are necessary to satisfy fickle customers.

The drop in the value of the dollar is another factor that makes U.S. manufacturing attractive again. Because of the recent devaluation of the dollar, material costs have risen dramatically compared to the cost of labor. U.S. manufacturing costs are not much higher, and in some cases lower, than those in Europe and some countries in the Pacific Rim.

It is also difficult to develop a partnership with an overseas supplier because of communication problems, national design conventions, national technical standards, and quality problems. With the increased importance of Just-In-Time delivery, the greater the distance the supplier is from the customer, the more chances there are for problems to occur. Problems tend to multiply each time material crosses a border or changes hands.

Offshore buying also makes communication more difficult. Engineering design changes have to be handled carefully. Imported products may have to be tested and inspected to assure they meet quality specifications and quantity requirements of the sales contracts. Testing is expensive and time-consuming. Also the problems of erratic quality, uncertain production schedules, and trade politics are deterrents to offshore sourcing.[2]

Short product development cycles also favor domestic purchasing over offshore sourcing. Partnering and simultaneous engineering require that the supplier works closely with customer teams. Offshore suppliers want frozen designs, which are a thing of the past. As product models and components change, domestic suppliers are in the best position to adapt quickly.

In many instances, customer and supplier integration favors a single source domestic partner. It is difficult to integrate suppliers of the same product located in different parts of the world into the customer's product development team. Of course, this assumes that the customer is surrounded by suppliers who know more about the supplied part than the customer does.

Currency Fluctuations

Even such a seemingly inconsequential issue as currency fluctuation has aggravated the risks of offshore sourcing and has created risks that did not exist several years ago. The price paid for imported material is affected by volatile exchange rates when payment is in the supplier's currency, and when there is a lag between the time a contract is signed and payment is made.

Buyers are required to learn and use a whole new set of tactics. Purchasing organizations are speculating in futures, writing orders denominated in U.S. dollars, writing orders fixed to a set valuation, and using sources in different countries to avoid being linked to the fluctuations of any one currency.[3]

This problem can be eliminated or at least alleviated if the supplier base is close to the final assembly plant and in the country where the product is marketed.

IT'S STILL DIFFICULT

Not all sourcing can be done domestically as we become economically interdependent with the rest of the world, however. More and more countries specify a level of domestic value content before a product can be sold in a local market. U.S. business will have to develop a wider perspective and a new set of skills.

The ability of U.S. companies to compete is also constrained by parochial attitudes. Until several years ago, managers could safely make marketing, sourcing, and design decisions while living in the United States. A foreign assignment was the equivalent of being sent to corporate Siberia. It was believed that to be out of sight was to be out of mind. So, foreign assignments were avoided.

Can we adapt easily? No, but we must. Achieving a global sourcing perspective and adapting to new conditions seem to be easier for Europeans and the Japanese. They have spent years in different parts of the world setting up manufacturing, design, distribution, and marketing networks. Often, foreign operations experience was a prerequisite for promotion in the home country.

Global sourcing and a global outlook are especially difficult for U.S. buyers. In an earlier time, our economy dominated the world and our business practices were universally mimicked. For example, when negotiating with foreign suppliers, U.S. business people in general tended to:

- Expect foreign business people to act and think like they did.
- Make quick on the spot decisions.
- Be precise when negotiating.
- Become informal too quickly.
- Consider rank less important than ability.

Now, Japanese financial presence and influence are pervasive. Their business practices are different than ours. Personal relationships are particularly important to Japanese business people and we must be flexible to recognize the differences and adapt to them. For example, the Japanese usually:

- Move more slowly through the negotiation process, relying on the whole organization to make decisions.
- Are more comfortable and tend to use silence as a negotiating tactic.
- Remain formal throughout the negotiating process.
- Try to focus on group harmony.
- Regard organizational rank as much more important than individual ability.[4]

Now, things are changing. MBA programs emphasize international business curricula; foreign language attendance is growing; leading U.S. business journals focus on the globalization of business; and a successful foreign assignment is a sign of a manager's maturity, often leading to upward mobility.

MILITARY PROCUREMENT

In this book, commercial purchasing practices have been emphasized. There is a growing tendency to apply commercial procurement practices to the public sector. The end of the Cold War has its price, which is that military contractors who have lived in a cost-driven environment must now live in a world of commercial competitiveness. Military contractors have to learn to speak a new language that includes such words as customer service, product quality, on budget, cost competitiveness, and product reliability. The following discusses several of the market-driven changes occurring in federal procurement.

Federal procurement and public-sector purchasing traditionally focused on process, procedures, and fairness more than the result of the purchasing efforts. Quality, delivery, and accountability were not significant compared to the front-end system price. Customer satisfaction and continuous quality improvement were also low priorities. Many believe that the focus on detailed procedures and specifications has made public-sector purchasing and its contractors non competitive in a global economy.[5]

LACK OF COMPETITIVENESS

Voluminous, rigid, and indecipherable bid documents tend to restrict competitiveness. Technical writers intend them to be clear, complete, and concise. Rigid specifications, however preclude considering products that are functionally comparable to those specified, thereby reducing the number of prospective suppliers.

Also, competition among contractors is based largely on price and does not consider or emphasize commercial factors such as quality, reliability, ease of use, aesthetics, delivery, or life-cycle costs.[6]

Another restriction to competitiveness is the requirement for sealed public bids in excess of a certain amount of money. The process ties public agencies to a supplier or a product the buyer may not prefer and leaves little negotiating latitude. The buyer usually cannot negotiate better terms and conditions, such as continuous improvement, better delivery, or lower pricing.[7]

Contractors counter that they need the stability of long-term contracts because they must track constant changes in regulatory laws, which makes the federal procurement environment inherently unstable and risky.[8]

ACQUISITION OF ARMS

An area of waste and sometimes fraud has been the acquisition of multiyear, multibillion dollar military systems. The lengthy acquisition timelines of these systems subject them to numerous and changing political agendas.

The acquisition of arms has become a high-profile endeavor as a result of waste, fraud, and mismanagement publicity. Problems, abuses, and inefficiencies in public-sector purchasing tend to be magnified in military procurement because of the vast sums of money involved. Recently, the Under Secretary of Defense for Acquisition estimated that the Pentagon wastes $40 billion annually through inefficient buying, designing, and manufacturing.

Pundits counter that procurement problems are a normal result of the complex nature of military hardware, as well as the high stakes involved. Military purchasing has hovered around $300 billion for several years. Compared to the overall military procurement budget, the extent of proven fraud is relatively small. Perceptions are damaging, however, when reputable blue-chip companies plead guilty to abuse charges.

DOD MONITORING

The Department of Defense has a costly but essential oversight structure for detecting fraud and mismanagement by contractors or their employees. In 1982, DOD named its first inspector general and the Department of Justice established its own defense purchasing fraud unit. Recently, there has been an increase in fraud investigations and convictions. Offenses include bribery of public officials, bid rigging, theft of government property, product substitution, and misuse of government property or service.

To combat these abuses, the Pentagon now employs more then 11,000 auditors and about the same number of investigators and inspectors. While there have been celebrated cases of whistle blowing, the Department of Justice and DOD have seemingly not been able to eliminate abuses.[9]

REFORMING THE PENTAGON

In light of the domestic budget deficits, the level of military procurement fraud and waste is unacceptable to the American people. In the 1990s, U.S. leadership will have to identify worldwide threats and develop a defense force capable of meeting these threats.

During the past several years, DOD procurement officials have attempted to administer new regulations for defense contractors. Some regulations have been implemented in an attempt to make defense contractors more competitive. The Packard Commission, named after its chairman, was a presidential group commissioned to review and recommend changes in the DOD procurement. The Packard Commission recommended the following: create a purchasing czar to streamline the acquisition process; reorganize the purchasing and auditing organization; develop realistic specifications and simpler procedures; expand the use of commercial products; and increase commercial style competition by emphasizing quality and performance as well as price.[10]

The perception of a need for a vast military system is changing to the perception of one that is particularly suited to meet specific needs quickly, such as the war in the Middle East. Also, there is a need to take these monies and pay off budgetary debts and reinvest in domestic infrastructure.

OPPORTUNITIES AND RISKS

These marketplace challenges have created risks and opportunities that will result in organizational, supplier, and people shakeups in the 1990s.

FOREIGN MANUFACTURERS

Having purchased, produced, and sold products in a global economy, foreign manufacturers understand better than U.S. management the urgency for competitively priced, high-quality products and services and the resulting rewards of partnering.

Many foreign companies are transplanting entire operations, including organizational practices, to the U.S. Many offshore companies are also buying American companies to gain a foothold in the world's largest market. The resulting intense foreign competition has chased many U.S. manufacturers out of primary and smaller secondary markets as more foreign firms have encroached into these markets.

In the automotive industry, offshore companies have transferred their own successful operational methods and management practices to U.S. transplants. Usually, management practices are not transferred wholesale without adapting to local and regional practices.

Whether it is the Nissan Smyrna plant, the Sharp electronics plant, quality is uniformly high, and labor costs are contained. Suppliers are considered an extension of the customer's plant and have similar production and quality systems in place. Corporate democracy is visible in terms of management and labor, and exempt employees have similar uniforms, eat in the same cafeteria, and don't have reserved parking spaces.[11]

JAPANESE PRACTICES

In Japan, small contractors or job shops are highly integrated into their customer's manufacturing, engineering, and quality systems. One recent study asserts that the customer-supplier relationship is more important than employment policies, management attitudes, and cultural traditions in accounting for Japanese competitive success.

Managers in large Japanese firms are actively involved in their suppliers' improvement efforts by continuously monitoring and improving processes at their suppliers' facilities. Toyota is a prime example of this close relationship. Toyota personnel actively supervise such supplier areas as facilities development, quality control, financing, and production scheduling for subcontractors.[12]

Experts believe this Japanese experience can be adapted to U.S. manufacturers and their suppliers. It is being tried at New United Motor Manufacturing Inc. (NUMMI) and at the Honda Marysville plants. NUMMI is a joint venture between GM and Toyota Motor Corporation, and Honda in Marysville, Ohio, is a sole Honda venture. The plants were once part of an experiment to determine if Japanese manufacturing and management techniques could be implemented successfully in the United States, with a unionized workforce in NUMMI and in general with U.S. suppliers. In the short term, the plants have been stunningly successful, but the jury is still out on whether they will be the model of future U.S. manufacturing plants.[13]

JUST ANOTHER PASSING PHASE

In the future, having a companywide quality effort will become a necessary condition of business for most suppliers of major U.S., Pacific Rim, and European companies. The supplier base of most large organizations has gone through several downsizings. Many suppliers have had to implement a quality effort for several years in order to stay on the customer's approved bidder's list.

Some suppliers perceive the quality improvement mania as the newest passing management trend, just as quality circles, JIT (Just-In-Time), MRP (Material Requirement Planning), or CIM (Computer Integrated Manufacturing) have been. These management philosophies were considered the answer to managing better and more effectively. Money, time, and other resources were invested in these ideas but results were sometimes negligible. Many suppliers hoped these trends would go away and some did. This ostrich-like response to quality, however, can result in complete loss of business.

In the robust economy of the last eight years, large companies encouraged and induced participation in quality partnerships. Suppliers were needed to produce critical parts. Often, the customer provided training and financial inducements. As the economy slows and many companies want to work only with worldclass suppliers, the messages have turned from encouraging to requiring participation in these continuous improvement efforts.

As you can imagine, the supplier response is mixed. Some see the opportunities—more business, reduced internal costs and enhanced competitiveness. Some fume and reluctantly say "OK, you're the customer." Others may be heard saying:

"This is supplier coercion, the two-by-four approach to supplier management."

"This will kill supplier partnering."

"This is unfair."

"Competing for the Natonal Quality Award will not improve product quality or service delivery."

From the customer's (purchasing's) point of view, such remarks as follow can be heard:

"We have invested in quality. We have encouraged you, the supplier, to develop higher quality levels, quality management systems, and higher service levels for years. Now, we want to see measurable improvement."

"We are worldclass. And we want to deal with worldclass suppliers."

"We are the customer. We want to compete in the world economy. We source a large percentage of our sales dollar. Our suppliers are an important element of our competitiveness equation."

Often, the biggest obstacle to supplier partnering is in the supplier's upper management. These managers may look upon the quality push as a passing fancy, here today and gone tomorrow. This is especially prevalent in small, single-owner entrepreneurial companies. Small business owners tend to resent the imposition of controls or the investment in training.

What happens to suppliers that do not or are not able to comply? Suppliers are told that maintaining quality is a condition for future business dealings. Suppliers that do not invest in companywide continuous improvement may exit certain business lines or change ownership; plants may shut; and product lines may be pared. Often, to comply, new equipment has to be purchased and installed, people have to be retrained, and a new cultural and organizational system has to evolve.

SUPPLIER SHAKEOUT

The United States has experienced an extended bull market. In this expansion, partnerships have been slow to get off the ground, largely because the market has favored suppliers. The demand for products and services has been so great that even marginal suppliers received business.

The devaluation of the dollar at first increased exports of commercial products. The military buildup also increased demand for military products. Quality and continuous improvement were not urgent to customers who simply needed products. They also were not urgent concerns to suppliers who had a guaranteed market for their products. Also, many medium and small suppliers did not feel the need for quality and continuous improvement because they sold to intermediate manufacturers and did not have to compete directly against West European or Japanese firms.

In the early 1990s, some form of economic contraction is inevitable. It may be a breather until the next business expansion or it may be a prolonged recession.

Regardless of the economic future, an accelerated supplier shakeout will take place and surpass the reductions in the supplier base that have already occurred. Suppliers that have been cooperative and worked with customers to develop continuous improvement partnerships will be retained. In some cases, customers will retain only those suppliers that have achieved preferred-partnership status. Others won't be so lucky and will be dropped. Suppliers that have developed at least a rudimentary quality program will have an advantage in the competitive 1990s.

NOTES

[1] Lawrence Kokotow, "The realities of Far East Procurement," *Purchasing World*, October 1986, pp. 37–39.

[2] Kevin McDermott, "Made in the USA: You Can Go Home Again," *D&B Reports*, March/April 1987, pp. 22–25.

[3] Jeff Perlman, "Devalued Dollar Prompts Catalogers to Develop New Sourcing Methods," *Catalog Age*, February 1989, pp. 36–38.

[4] Eugene Mendonsa, "Seven Deadly Sins of Purchasing Overseas," *Purchasing World*, March 1987, pp. 90–91.

[5] John Trinkaus, "Competitive Advocacy and Spare Parts," *Journal of Purchasing and Materials Management*," Winter 1984, pp. 22–26.

[6] Louis DeRose, "Government Rigidity Fouls Competition," *Purchasing World*, October 1986, p. 28.

[7] Joseph Herrod, "Public Purchasing: Too Many Restrictions," *Purchasing World*, August 1987, pp. 79–80.

[8] Gary Stix, "Competition Alters Equation for Industry," IEEE *Spectrum*, November 1988, pp. 47–51.

[9] Glenn Zorpette, "Government Oversight: Fighting Waste and Fraud," *IEEE Spectrum*, November 1988, pp. 44–47.

[10] Daniel Gottlieb, "Defense Buying Hits the Fan," *Purchasing*, September 1988, pp. 91–93.

[11] Nathaniel Gilbert, "Foreign Companies Use Democracy to Prosper in the US," *Management Review*, July 1988, pp. 25–29.

[12] Allan Baillie, "Subcontracting Based on Integrated Standards: The Japanese Approach," *Journal of Purchasing and Materials Management*, Spring 1986, pp. 17–22.

[13] Lee Branst, Labor/Management Participation: "The NUMMI Experience," *Quality Progress*, April 1988, pp. 30–34.

Index

OTHER IRWIN *Professional Publishing* TITLES OF INTEREST TO YOU

COMPETING IN WORLD CLASS MANUFACTURING
America's 21st Century Challenge
National Center for Manufacturing Sciences

Discover how a firm commitment to quality and the customer affects every aspect of your organization. *Competing in World Class Manufacturing* shows you how to improve your firm's quality in product, process, and service. You'll learn how to respond to the need for increased flexibility and quicker response time so you can satisfy customer demand.
ISBN: 1-55623-401-5 $42.50

MEASURING UP
Charting Pathways to Manufacturing Excellence
The Business One Irwin/APICS Series in Production Management
Robert W. Hall, H. Thomas Johnson, and Peter B.B. Turney

This is the ultimate guide for manufacturing executives and managers looking to improve their overall competitiveness. *Measuring Up* covers both operational and cost measurement so you can improve costing for better results, manage your organization for continual improvement, and measure the proper functions to ensure excellence.
ISBN: 1-55623-359-0 $42.50

THE NEW PERFORMANCE CHALLENGE
Measuring Operations for World-Class Competition
The Business One Irwin/APICS Series in Production Management
J. Robb Dixon, Alfred J. Nanni, and Thomas E. Vollmann

The authors provide timely, practical, and powerful solutions to the performance measurement problems facing manufacturing firms in the new competitive environment. This book includes specific examples of how some of today's *Fortune* 500 companies are profiting from effective performance measurement.
ISBN: 1-55623-301-9 $42.50

PLANNING FOR QUALITY, PRODUCTIVITY, AND COMPETITIVE POSITION
Howard S. Gitlow

The authors show you how to increase productivity, employee morale, and profits. You'll find step-by-step guidelines for gathering and evaluating valuable information from employees, customers, and suppliers that are essential to implementing a successful, time-sequenced action plan.
ISBN: 1-55623-357-4 $39.95

TIME-BASED COMPETITION
The Next Battle Ground in American Manufacturing
Joseph D. Blackburn, Editor

Discover how time compression can reduce costs and improve quality in your firm. Blackburn shows you how to use fewer clerical hours to process orders and improve customer response time. This book demonstrates how to move finished products out the door more quickly and maintain low inventory levels.
ISBN: 1-55623-321-3 $42.50

Prices Subject to Change Without Notice.
Available in Fine Bookstores and Libraries Everywhere.